THE BOLD, THE YOUNG, AND THE MURDERED

A MURDER MYSTERY COMEDY BY
Don Zolidis

The Bold, The Young, and The Murdered (1st ed. - 07.11.11) - boldtheyoungDgm
Copyright © 2011 Don Zolidis

ALL RIGHTS RESERVED

Copyright Protection. This play (the "Play") is fully protected under the copyright laws of the United States of America and all countries with which the United States has reciprocal copyright relations, whether through bilateral or multilateral treaties or otherwise, and including, but not limited to, all countries covered by the Pan-American Copyright Convention, the Universal Copyright Convention, and the Berne Convention.

Reservation of Rights. All rights to this Play are strictly reserved, including, without limitation, professional and amateur stage performance rights; motion picture, recitation, lecturing, public reading, radio broadcasting, television, video, and sound recording rights; rights to all other forms of mechanical or electronic reproduction now known or yet to be invented, such as CD-ROM, CD-I, DVD, photocopying, and information storage and retrieval systems; and the rights of translation into non-English languages.

Performance Licensing and Royalty Payments. Amateur and stock performance rights to this Play are controlled exclusively by Playscripts, Inc. ("Playscripts"). No amateur or stock production groups or individuals may perform this Play without obtaining advance written permission from Playscripts. Required royalty fees for performing this Play are specified online at the Playscripts website (www.playscripts.com). Such royalty fees may be subject to change without notice. Although this book may have been obtained for a particular licensed performance, such performance rights, if any, are not transferable. Required royalties must be paid every time the Play is performed before any audience, whether or not it is presented for profit and whether or not admission is charged. All licensing requests and inquiries concerning amateur and stock performance rights should be addressed to Playscripts (see contact information on opposite page).

Inquiries concerning all other rights should be addressed to Playscripts, as well; such inquiries will be communicated to the author and the author's agent, as applicable.

Restriction of Alterations. There shall be no deletions, alterations, or changes of any kind made to the Play, including the changing of character gender, the cutting of dialogue, the cutting of music, or the alteration of objectionable language, unless directly authorized by Playscripts. The title of the Play shall not be altered.

Author Credit. Any individual or group receiving permission to produce this Play is required to give credit to the author as the sole and exclusive author of the Play. This obligation applies to the title page of every program distributed in connection with performances of the Play, and in any instance that the title of the Play appears for purposes of advertising, publicizing, or otherwise exploiting the Play and/or a production thereof. The name of the author must appear on a separate line, in which no other name appears, immediately beneath the title and of a font size at least 50% as large as the largest letter used in the title of the Play. No person, firm, or entity may receive credit larger or more prominent than that accorded the author. The name of the author may not be abbreviated or otherwise altered from the form in which it appears in this Play.

Publisher Attribution. All programs, advertisements, and other printed material distributed or published in connection with the amateur or stock production of the Play shall include the following notice:

Produced by special arrangement with Playscripts, Inc.
(www.playscripts.com)

Prohibition of Unauthorized Copying. Any unauthorized copying of this book or excerpts from this book is strictly forbidden by law. Except as otherwise permitted by applicable law, no part of this book may be reproduced, stored in a retrieval system, or transmitted in any form, by any means now known or yet to be invented, including, without limitation, photocopying or scanning, without prior permission from Playscripts.

Statement of Non-affiliation. This Play may include references to brand names and trademarks owned by third parties, and may include references to public figures. Playscripts is not necessarily affiliated with these public figures, or with the owners of such trademarks and brand names. Such references are included solely for parody, political comment, or other permitted purposes.

Permissions for Sound Recordings and Musical Works. This Play may contain directions calling for the performance of a portion, or all, of a musical work *not included in the Play's score*, or performance of a sound recording of such a musical work. Playscripts has not obtained permissions to perform such works. The producer of this Play is advised to obtain such permissions, if required in the context of the production. The producer is directed to the websites of the U.S. Copyright Office (www.copyright.gov), ASCAP (www.ascap.com), BMI (www.bmi.com), and NMPA (www.nmpa.org) for further information on the need to obtain permissions, and on procedures for obtaining such permissions.

The Rules in Brief

1) Do NOT perform this Play without obtaining prior permission from Playscripts, and without paying the required royalty.

2) Do NOT photocopy, scan, or otherwise duplicate any part of this book.

3) Do NOT alter the text of the Play, change a character's gender, delete any dialogue, cut any music, or alter any objectionable language, unless explicitly authorized by Playscripts.

4) DO provide the required credit to the author(s) and the required attribution to Playscripts in all programs and promotional literature associated with any performance of this Play.

For more details on these and other rules, see the opposite page.

Copyright Basics

This Play is protected by United States and international copyright law. These laws ensure that authors are rewarded for creating new and vital dramatic work, and protect them against theft and abuse of their work.

A play is a piece of property, fully owned by the author, just like a house or car. You must obtain permission to use this property, and must pay a royalty fee for the privilege—whether or not you charge an admission fee. Playscripts collects these required payments on behalf of the author.

Anyone who violates an author's copyright is liable as a copyright infringer under United States and international law. Playscripts and the author are entitled to institute legal action for any such infringement, which can subject the infringer to actual damages, statutory damages, and attorneys' fees. A court may impose statutory damages of up to $150,000 for willful copyright infringements. U.S. copyright law also provides for possible criminal sanctions. Visit the website of the U.S. Copyright Office (www.copyright.gov) for more information.

THE BOTTOM LINE: If you break copyright law, you are robbing a playwright and opening yourself to expensive legal action. Follow the rules, and when in doubt, ask us.

Playscripts, Inc.
450 Seventh Ave, Suite 809
New York, NY 10123

toll-free phone: 1-866-NEW-PLAY
email: info@playscripts.com
website: www.playscripts.com

Cast of Characters

JAKE STRONG, played by MORRIS NYBORG
SEBASTIAN STRONG, played by BILL WILEY
VALENCIO DI CARPATHIO, played by JOHN BURKE
MONA JEFFRIES, played by CYBIL DANE
EILEEN SILVERSTEDT, played by AMY WHITE
JESSICA SILVERSTEDT, played by DANIELLE FARRIS
DOCTOR WILLIAM BRADLEY, played by TYLER TRIPODO
SEQUOIYA, played by LILY BAUMGARTNER

Other characters:
OLI, the director
KAITLIN, stage manager
KERI, the intern
BROOKE, the camerawoman
MILES, the producer

Character Notes

Eight actors play the parts of eight characters inside the long-running Soap Opera, *The Bold and the Young*.

OLI, KAITLIN, BROOKE, and MILES may be either gender. The names may be changed as follows:

OLI stays the same
KAITLIN is TODD
BROOKE is LOUIS
MILES is MARY

Setting

The television set of *The Bold and the Young*. Present Day.

Acknowledgments

The Bold, the Young, and the Murdered was originally performed by the Tri-Arts Academy in Muskego, Wisconsin, on May 21, 2011, with the following cast:

JAKE STRONG / MORRIS NYBORG	Matthew Wiemer
SEBASTIAN STRONG / BILL WILEY	Connor Loessin
VALENCIO DI CARPATHIO/ JOHN BURKE	Josh Wilke
MONA JEFFRIES / CYBIL DANE	Sadie Stoiber
EILEEN SILVERSTEDT / AMY WHITE	Lyssa Lee
JESSICA SILVERSTEDT/ DANIELLE FARRIS	Alyson Robinson
DOCTOR WILLIAM BRADLEY/ TYLER TRIPODO	Sam Robinson
SEQUOIYA / LILY BAUMGARTNER	Beekah Madia
OLI	Brittany Zimmer
KAITLIN	Lauren Wundrock
KERI	Amanda Smith
BROOKE	Maija Lee
MILES	Robert Somers

The Bold, The Young, and The Murdered, Spanaway Lake High School, Spanaway Lake, Washington (2011).

The Bold, the Young, and the Murdered

by Don Zolidis

ACT I

(Soothing piano theme music. Lights up on the set of The Bold and the Young. *A room in the mansion of* VALENCIO DI CARPATHIO, *60ish, who reclines on a couch with a glass of sherry in his hand.* VALENCIO *is well-dressed, with silver hair, and is pretty obviously evil. He also speaks with a mysterious Eastern European accent.* JAKE STRONG, *35ish, and devastatingly handsome, enters. He speaks with a very handsome accent [mostly this involves trying to sound really tough all the time]. Just off-stage, and barely visible to the audience, are* BROOKE, *the camerawoman, and* OLI, *the director. For the moment, they are silent.)*

VALENCIO. Ah, Jake Strong. How nice of you to join me.

(He sips his sherry evilly.)

JAKE STRONG. What do you want from me, Valencio Di Carpathio?

VALENCIO. Why are you so suspicious? Can't I invite my friend over for a nice little chat? Sherry?

JAKE STRONG. The last time I touched your Sherry I ended up in a mental hospital for three months. Then you convinced my half-brother to steal my father's fortune. So I think I'll decline the sherry this time. Even though it looks pretty good and I'm quite thirsty from riding my motorcycle over here.

VALENCIO. As you wish, Jake Strong. As you wish.

(He sips the sherry again, perhaps even more evilly than before.)

JAKE STRONG. I'll ask you again, what do you want?

VALENCIO. Have a seat.

JAKE STRONG. The last time I sat in one of your chairs I was poisoned by an Amazonian tree frog and woke up hallucinating in a Nigerian diamond mine, so I think I'll stand, thank you very much. Although I appreciate the sentiment.

VALENCIO. Very well. Although standing can get…

(Dramatic pause.)

VALENCIO. ...uncomfortable.

JAKE STRONG. So can my fist to your face.

VALENCIO. Oh please. Must you always make these threats? I'm an old man, Jake Strong. I may not last long. In fact, there is the very real possibility that I'm dying of something very secretive. I don't know yet, and we might not find out for some time, but it's a definite possibility. So I'm going to make amends. You remember your wife, Nina?

JAKE STRONG. YOU MONSTER WHAT HAVE YOU DONE WITH HER?!

VALENCIO. I just asked you if you remembered her.

JAKE STRONG. Oh. Yes. We're quite happy together. She's the light of my life.

VALENCIO. I'm glad to hear that.

JAKE STRONG. What are you getting at, Valencio?

VALENCIO. Oh nothing. Except maybe...you know there is something in her history you might not know.

JAKE STRONG. If it's the part about her spending a year in clown college after high school, I know all about that. She was young. And she liked big shoes. They brainwashed her. If I ever get my hands on those clowns...

VALENCIO. Oh no this is something completely different.

JAKE STRONG. I also happen to know about her evil twin sister, Deborah, who you brainwashed into thinking she was my wife while Nina was undergoing a secretive nose job in South America. And who later became pregnant, but lost the baby and was kidnapped by pirates and hasn't been seen again.

VALENCIO. I forgot about that time. That was fun. No I have something even more disturbing to tell you. Your wife, Nina, is my daughter.

JAKE STRONG. Noooooo!

OLI. *(From off-stage:)* CUT!

> *(JAKE and VALENCIO drop out of character immediately. JAKE puts on glasses and becomes MORRIS NYBORG; his voice changes completely. VALENCIO drops his accent and becomes JOHN BURKE, a crotchety old guy.)*

JOHN. Could we please turn the heat on in here, I'm freezing my tuckus off.

MORRIS. How was that, Oli?

(OLI *leaps up on to the set.* OLI *is a ball of energy.*)

OLI. Having a good day, Morris?

MORRIS. I've got a little bit of a cold right now, but I'm not really—

OLI. I don't really care. Okay? Good.

JOHN. Anybody got soup?

OLI. Nobody's got soup, John.

JOHN. I demand soup.

OLI. No you can't demand anything—

JOHN. I've been on this show for forty-seven years and I want soup. Cream of asparagus. Cream of asparagus or I go home right now.

MORRIS. Was I not gritting my teeth enough, was that it? I've got a problem with one of my incisors, so I'm not really able to clench my jaw like I used—

OLI. Morris. Morris. Morris. Morris.

MORRIS. What?

OLI. Shut up. All right listen up. That was wretched, okay? Wretched. Where was the intensity? Where was the drama?

JOHN. There'd be drama if I had soup.

OLI. Hey hey attention up here Grandpa. You get soup after you nail the scene, all right?

JOHN. It's in my contract that I get soup whenever I want—

OLI. Do you want me to have Valencio's personality downloaded into a computer again so I can fire you and replace with you with a See-n-Say? Cause I can do it. All right? We're doing the scene again.

MORRIS. The whole thing?

OLI. Yes the whole thing!

MORRIS. Aw jeez.

JOHN. This is ridiculous. I want double soup now.

(KAITLIN, *the stage manager, rushes over to* OLI.)

OLI. There's no such thing as double—what is it, sweetheart?

KAITLIN. My name's not sweetheart, it's Kaitlin.

OLI. Ask yourself one question: do I care?

KAITLIN. I just got the—

OLI. The answer is no.

st got the ratings for last week.

hands them to OLI.)

Jang it. I thought the plotline with the escaped mental patie... ...h the poisonous fruit tree would really bring in the viewers.

KAITLIN. I don't think people really understood the radioactive mango thing—

OLI. I'm not asking for your opinion, all right babe? Why don't you do your job and set up the props again. We're re-doing the scene.

KAITLIN. Fine.

(KAITLIN *rushes to re-fill the glass of Sherry.*)

JOHN. We haven't addressed the soup issue.

OLI. There is no soup issue!

JOHN. There is most definitely a soup issue!

MORRIS. John, we'll deal with it after, okay? But before we do that, can I make some adjustments to my costume?

OLI. No.

KAITLIN. Places! I think.

OLI. *(To* BROOKE:*)* Brooke, you ready?

BROOKE. No.

OLI. You're not ready?

BROOKE. I just stand here, what do you think?

OLI. Love the attitude, Brooke. And, from the top, and Five Four Three Two…

(*Lights brighten on the stage again.* JOHN *and* MORRIS *resume their characters perfectly, except this time they are even more passionate and intense. Extremely, extremely intense.*)

VALENCIO. Ah, Jake Strong. How nice of you…to join me.

(*He sips his sherry evilly.*)

JAKE STRONG. What do you want from me, Valencio…Di Carpathio?

VALENCIO. Why are you so suspicious? Can't I invite my friend over for a nice little chat?

(*Dramatic pause.*)

Sherry?

JAKE STRONG. The last time I touched your Sherry I ended up in a mental hospital for three months. Then you convinced my half-brother to steal my family's fortune. So I think I'll decline the sherry this time. Even though it looks pretty good and I'm quite thirsty from riding my motorcycle

(Dramatic pause.)

over here.

VALENCIO. As you wish, Jake Strong. As you wish.

(He sips the sherry again, perhaps even more evilly than before.)

I would offer you soup but I don't have soup.

JAKE STRONG. I don't want your…soup.

VALENCIO. Too bad. Because I could really use some…soup.

OLI. CUT!

(They break out of character.)

What in the heck are you doing?!

MORRIS. *(Putting glasses on:)* I really wanted to fill out the backside of these pants, so I was kind of standing more like this—is there a way we could sew some padding—

OLI. Not you, idiot.

JOHN. Do you think you scare me? I've seen fourteen directors on this show, okay? I'm going to my trailer and having my soup and if you don't like it you can put it in a letter and mail it to someone who cares.

OLI. No one writes letters any more you fossil!

JOHN. Bye.

(JOHN leaves.)

OLI. That's the way you want to play, huh? Your character is going to end up dead one of these days! You know that! Dead!

(JOHN returns.)

JOHN. My character has been killed nine times already, all right? I'm not scared about ten. I keep coming back.

(He leaves again.)

(MORRIS approaches, holding a copy of Soap Opera Digest.)

MORRIS. The reason I'm concerned is that I'm not on the list of daytime TV's sexiest hunks—and I was on it last year, and I'm wondering what happened—so I'm thinking we need to increase my appeal,

...what if we did some swimsuit scenes where we got a...

...is, as much as I appreciate your soul-crushing insecuri... ...have a show to do. And your rear end is not the only draw on t... show—

MORRIS. But I'm saying—

OLI. Quiet. We're moving on. Scene Two!

KAITLIN. Places for Scene Two! We need Eileen and Jessica! Eileen and Jessica!

>(DANIELLE, *20ish, enters as* KAITLIN *rearranges the set for Eileen's kitchen. [This can be done by simply changing locations, or removing the couch and replacing it with a different piece of furniture. It doesn't have to look great.]*)

DANIELLE. Oh my Gosh I am so excited to be here! This is so wonderful everyone!

OLI. Thanks.

DANIELLE. Brooke, you just look lovely today!

BROOKE. I'm in the dark.

DANIELLE. It really works for you, though. In a good way.

OLI. Where's Eileen?

DANIELLE. She's in her dressing room. She is so just so talented, don't you think? I just love her!

KAITLIN. Eileen! Places!

>(AMY *enters in costume, holding her coffee and grumbling.*)

AMY. What.

KAITLIN. Places for Scene Two!

AMY. Fine.

OLI. All right ladies, let's get some fur flying in this one okay?

AMY. Am I some kind of animal to you?

OLI. No I just—I want conflict.

AMY. Like a catfight, right? Cause I'm a woman? Is that what you think?

DANIELLE. I'm a woman! Real fur flying! Got it. Meow.

AMY. You're a twit.

DANIELLE. That's so nice of you to say that.

KAITLIN. Okay everyone. Places!

AMY. Sure.

DANIELLE. Um...I forgot where places was.

KAITLIN. You're coming in the room.

DANIELLE. Awesome. Got it.

KAITLIN. Amy you're—

AMY. *(Rude:)* I know where I am. Thank you.

OLI. And five four three two—

(Soap Opera music again.)

(EILEEN SILVERSTEDT, the heroine, [played by AMY] is sunnily cleaning up, perhaps humming a sweet little song as JESSICA, an angry teenager, [played by DANIELLE] enters in a huff.)

EILEEN. Oh you're home!

JESSICA. Hello, mother.

EILEEN. I was just cleaning up a little bit for dinner. You said you were bringing your new fiancé.

JESSICA. Clean all you want, it won't make a difference.

EILEEN. Sweetheart—

JESSICA. Don't you understand, mother? You've lost. The game is over.

EILEEN. I just want you to be happy.

JESSICA. Do you?

EILEEN. Of course I do honey, you've been through so much, with the kidnapping by pirates, and the mind erasing by that Swedish psychiatrist, and the complete personality change you've undergone, I'm just glad that everything is back to normal.

JESSICA. I'm glad to hear that, mother. I'd like you to meet my fiancé.

(SEBASTIAN STRONG [played by BILL WILEY], wearing an eyepatch, but still looking devilishly handsome, enters.)

EILEEN. *(Gasping:)* Sebastian Strong!

SEBASTIAN. Nice to see you again, Eileen.

EILEEN. It can't be! This isn't possible!

JESSICA. We're in love, mother. We'll be married in three days.

EILEEN. You can't do this! You don't understand who this man is!

ve changed, Eileen. I'm no longer the man who poisoned Although I will say, their screams were exquisite.

oldfish don't scream!

S~~ IAN. Yours did.

EILEEN. You monster!

(To JESSICA:)

Darling I won't let you do this.

JESSICA. You just don't get it, do you, mother? You're the monster, not Sebastian! I don't care that he has an eye patch, I wouldn't care if he wore two eye patches and stumbled around and bumped into things, I love him! And I'll be the one looking out his passenger side rear view mirror so he can see objects that are closer than they appear to be!

EILEEN. I raised you better than this!

JESSICA. You didn't raise me, the nanny raised me!

EILEEN. HOW DARE YOU?!

JESSICA. This relationship is over!

EILEEN. You can't say that!

JESSICA. I just did!

EILEEN. You ungrateful child!

JESSICA. You're not my mother any more, do you hear me?! Do you hear me? Next time I see you you'll just be some nice lady in a kitchen who likes to do the dusting every once in a while and occasionally bakes brownies. And I might take a brownie or two, but… I'll. Pay. You. For. Them. I'm leaving! And I'm not even going to have dinner! We'll go out to Kentucky Fried Chicken!

EILEEN. Their chicken is substandard!

JESSICA. That's good enough for me! Come fiancé!

(She exits. SEBASTIAN remains for a moment.)

SEBASTIAN. Oh one more thing.

(Dramatic pause.)

Would you like chicken…or fish at the wedding?

(He laughs evilly and exits.)

OLI. CUT!

(DANIELLE returns quickly to talk to AMY.)

DANIELLE. Oh my gosh you were so amazing in that, look at skin, I've got goosebumps!

AMY. Yeah, whatever.

    (BILL WILEY *comes back in as* AMY *addresses* OLI.)

Can I say something other than "their chicken is substandard"? That's a really stupid line.

OLI. You're a stupid line. And no we can't change the script!

AMY. How about their chicken is godawful?

OLI. No—just—

DANIELLE. Ooh! Causes cancer in rats!

BILL. *(To* DANIELLE:*)* Hey kid. That was spectacular.

DANIELLE. Really?

BILL. First-rate work. You know what I like about you? Your hair.

DANIELLE. I love my hair too!

BILL. How about you and me go in the other room and rehearse?

AMY. Bill—could you please refrain from hitting on the actresses for a moment?

BILL. Stuff it, Amy. You're just jealous.

AMY. Oh yeah I'm jealous of a washed-up has-been mediocre slimebag.

DANIELLE. What did you just call me?

AMY. Not you, idiot.

OLI. People! Hey! Save it for the cameras! All right, it's five o' clock and that means today is—

    (*The intern,* KERI, *sprints in.*)

KERI. Oli hold on!

OLI. Who are you again?

KERI. I'm Keri the intern, hi everyone. It's my first day!

DANIELLE. Hi!

    (*No one else acknowledges her presence.*)

KERI. I'm so excited to be here! I'm a huge fan of the show and this is such an amazing opportunity for me! I'm dreamed about this my whole life!

AMY. You've dreamed about being an intern on a Soap Opera. You need better dreams.

...ke a stepping stone for me—

...s your name—Carly—internships exist to give of the production staff something to do, all right? ...g anywhere.

...ut I have something important to say!

OLI. ...n you please spit it out because I'm about to die of boredom listening to you talk.

KERI. There's a guy here to talk to you—in a suit—um...Milo?

OLI. Miles?

KERI. That's it!

(A hush falls over everyone.)

He's like the excellent producer or something—

OLI. Executive producer, sweetheart. Aw dang it!

KAITLIN. Everyone get out here!

(MORRIS enters.)

MORRIS. I didn't think we were going back to that scene—

(LILY BAUMGARTNER, a young, troubled-looking woman, enters.)

LILY. Kaitlin. You don't have to yell. We all heard you.

KAITLIN. *(Yelling:)* Everyone get out here now!

JOHN. *(Off-stage:)* I'm still having my soup!

OLI. John get out here!

JOHN. *(Off-stage:)* I will throw your body in the river when I'm done with you!

(CYBIL, who has been on the show since it began, 50 years ago, enters, wearing a dressing gown. She's been on the show so long she has trouble distinguishing when she's on or off camera.)

CYBIL. Darlings, it's five o'clock and I'm beginning to turn into a pumpkin, so this better be quick! I also have to go home to feed President Bush and Laura Bush.

KERI. You have them trapped in your house?

CYBIL. Pomeranians. I also had one named Senator Arlen Spector.

KERI. What happened to him?

CYBIL. Her. She ran away. I don't like to speak about it. Kidnapped, really. Held for ransom. It was a dark night, and I received a phone call—

The Bold, the Young, and the Mur...

JOHN. We did that episode twelve years ago, Cybil.

CYBIL. Then I don't know what happened to my dog. I'm worried.

(TYLER *enters on a cell phone.*)

TYLER. *(Talking into the phone:)* Tell them I'm not doing it for less than 2 million. I don't care if Matt Damon is in the picture, that's my rate. Well I don't care Jimmy. It's not like I'm going to be doing soaps forever. Yeah, I know slumming it with the little people—have you talked to Spielberg? Well get him on the phone—

OLI. All right everyone look!

TYLER. *(To* OLI:*)* Do you mind?

(*Back into the phone:*)

Jimmy. Jimmy. I want two cases of mineral water in the trailer. Always. I drink one bottle, I want a new bottle instantly, got it? And aromatherapy candles. I know I don't have the part yet but when I do—

OLI. Tyler!

TYLER. *(To* OLI:*)* Try not to be rude, okay?

(*Back to the phone:*)

Nobody important. Like I was saying.

(OLI *grabs the phone and tosses it.* TYLER *stares at him.*)

Are you KIDDING me? Are you KIDDING ME? You just signed your death warrant, buddy. DEATH WARRANT.

OLI. Try it, poser. Have a seat everyone.

(JOHN *enters, with napkin.*)

How nice of you to join us, John.

JOHN. Hmph.

OLI. First things—

KERI. Hi I'm Keri I'm the new intern! This is my first day!

OLI. No that is not the first thing.

KERI. Oh I thought we were introducing ourselves.

DANIELLE. You're going to love it here, Keri!

BILL. You like to party?

OLI. Hey! HEY! Please.

CYBIL. Darlings! I need to make an announcement!

(*Everyone looks at her.*)

...py at night. Just so you know.

...e loopy during the day too.

...ow I met my first husband! It was a dark night, raining, the ghost of...

A. ... did that one twenty-eight years ago.

OLI. Okay, thanks for that. But what I'm trying to tell you is—

(MILES, *in a business suit, enters.*)

MILES. I'm glad you're all here.

KERI. Hi I'm Keri!

OLI. (*Changing personality suddenly:*) Oh hello sir how nice of you to join us. Let's give Miles a round of applause!

(DANIELLE *claps happily. She's alone.*)

MILES. I don't have a lot of time so I'll make this brief. I know you guys have been hearing a lot of rumors about the future of the show.

DANIELLE. There are rumors?

MILES. Most of them are true. Look—we're just not reaching our audience—so the network is thinking about killing the show.

BILL. What!

AMY. You can't do that!

TYLER. It's about time.

MILES. Hey hey—no need to get upset just cause you probably won't have jobs any more.

KERI. Do I still have a job?

OLI. Wait a minute! I know we've had a bad run lately but we can come back—we can do another story with cannibals, everybody loved that! We'll all get lost in South America or something—

MILES. Hey—

JOHN. You need us, suit boy. You think that hour slot every day is gonna fill itself. Ha!

MILES. This isn't 1954 anymore, grandpa. I can replace this show in five minutes with a cheaper soap opera made in China. They got entire script factories churning out low-cost, high quality television entertainment—You want to see efficiency on a set? They film three episodes a day. They pay their actors in birdseed and still everybody sings songs about how happy they are.

OLI. This is insane. You can't just—

MILES. Hey! Nothing's final yet. But unless you can show me some gain in productivity—

AMY. What are you talking about?

MILES. Here's the deal: You guys are the slowest-shooting soap out there.

OLI. That's because we do quality.

MILES. No it's because you argue about everything.

JOHN. That's not true!

AMY. Yes it is!

JOHN. I'll hunt you down!

MILES. You are proving my point. We can't afford to spend this much time on this show. You've got to speed it up. Here's the deal: give me a high quality, top-notch episode by tomorrow morning and I'll recommend that we keep the show running.

KAITLIN. We have to finish the show tonight?

JOHN. Oh come on I get cranky at night.

TYLER. You're cranky all the time!

JOHN. And I have a right to be!

BILL. And Amy gets less attractive as the night goes on. Trust me, I've been there. High five?

(No one gives BILL a high-five.)

MILES. Tough. Finish the show tonight. Or you're doomed.

OLI. We can do it!

KERI. Yes! Right?

DANIELLE. I'm with you!

CYBIL. This is just too much for me emotionally. What will I do if I don't have the show? I could go back into modeling—I'll have to get my headshots redone—

TYLER. I know a guy—top notch.

JOHN. This is ridiculous. I'm going home.

MILES. Nobody's going home. I've had the intern—

KERI. That's me!

MILES. Lock all the doors from the outside—we've sent all the other workers home—you're trapped here.

LILY. You know I've been quiet because I'm trying to be a pleasant person—it's a new thing my court-ordered therapists have suggested—but let me say a little something here:

MORRIS. Here we go.

LILY. Morris—Remember the time when I apologized for biting you in the arm and sending you to the hospital?

MORRIS. I think I have post-traumatic stress disorder from the apology.

LILY. Yeah well most of me has now denounced violence but there's still part of me that could be convinced, okay?

MORRIS. Shutting mouth.

KERI. *(Under her breath:)* I like her.

LILY. All right mister director man—

MILES. Producer—

LILY. Whatever. You think we come to work every day and don't act our hearts out, is that it? Look at John!

JOHN. Er?

LILY. As far as I'm concerned that man is acting personified! If you took the idea of acting and made it into a sixty year old man with gout and the occasional hernia and a strange need for soup, that would be it! And look at Amy there! She's maybe fifty years old already and she—

AMY. I'm thirty nine—

LILY. And she's getting old and disgusting and she's not nearly as attractive as she used to be and she's still here acting her guts out! And the rest of the people on the cast might not have enough talent to make it in Hollywood, but they have just enough talent for daytime TV! And that's good enough for the doctors' offices and Laundromats! And home-schooled kids! I say we have a good show! I say we have a great show! And if anyone has a problem with that I will kick you in the head until you think about it differently! Right everyone?!

(Everyone is confused. DANIELLE raises her hand.)

DANIELLE. I'm not quite sure what your point is. I like your tone though.

LILY. Here it is! I am not that stable! You do not want me in the rest of society! There's only one career where a person with as many personality disorders as me could possibly make a living! And that's acting! So if you take this away from me, I promise you, I will be the bag lady screaming outside your house at three in the morning! Okay? I know where you live!

MILES. And I know where you live!

KERI. I know where everyone lives!

(Everyone looks at her.)

Freedom of Information Act. You can find this stuff out.

MILES. Look, I'm on your side. I don't want a Chinese Soap Opera. They sing in that really weird way.

AMY. That's Chinese Opera.

CYBIL. My Pomeranians love Chinese Opera. Really gets 'em howling.

MILES. Either way. But you guys gotta show it to me. Otherwise, you're all fired. Except Danielle because I think I've got a spot for you in the Chinese show. If you can learn the language.

DANIELLE. I can totally do that! I have no standards at all!

BILL. Perfect.

MILES. That's what I like to hear. Until tomorrow then—Sayonara.

KAITLIN. That's Japanese.

MILES. Oh. Goodbye then. In Chinese.

(He leaves.)

(TYLER looks up from his iPad.)

TYLER. Wait, what's going on?

AMY. Oh wake up Tyler.

TYLER. I am awake, thank you very much, I just have more important things to think about: like myself and how awesome I am.

(He thinks about how awesome he is for a second.)

Nice.

OLI. We're all gonna get fired if we can't finish the shoot tonight.

TYLER. Okay. Thanks. Now I know.

OLI. All right gather round everyone. I'm not one for emotional speeches. But you know where I got my start?

JOHN. No. And I don't care either.

OLI. I was eight years old. My parents got me a video camera for Christmas—it ran on my imagination—but later I got a real one—I used to make movies in my room, little shows I'd put on, put my teddy bear in a dress—

JOHN. You're sick.

OLI. Put a stuffed duck in a tuxedo—stage a wedding between them, and then have a panda show up and just starting throwing punches—screaming and tearing at each other—sometimes I'd take my father's razor—he always used Bic disposables, and then I'd shave little parts out of my stuffed animals and say they were injured during the fight and I'd have them in a hospital with a frog doctor and the doctor would fall in love, but there'd be another frog who looked the same and was also in love—

AMY. Does this story have a point?

DANIELLE. Shh! What happened to the frog doctor?

OLI. My point is this: I am soap opera. When I'm in the shower in the morning I'm thinking about soap opera, when I'm having breakfast, I'm thinking about soap opera, when I'm asleep I'm having weird and disturbing dreams about soap opera—I don't have a wife, I don't have friends, I don't have anyone who loves me, I'm really kind of alone and sad in the world but I have this! Who's with me!?

KERI. I AM!

OLI. Okay. Good.

AMY. Can I change some of my lines?

OLI. NO YOU CAN'T CHANGE YOUR LINES!

AMY. I would not say the word substandard!

TYLER. Can I just say something here? I've had a great time working with you people but I'm really poised to be a lot more famous than everyone, so—

OLI. You're staying here!

TYLER. You just signed your DEATH WARRANT buddy!

(Everyone looks at him.)

It's a line from the film I'm auditioning for. *Death Warrant.* With Matt Damon.

MORRIS. And I'm insecure about my body image!

OLI. Shut up all of you! We're doing this! We're doing the show! No one is going anywhere until we are all dead or this episode is finished! Got it? Places for scene three!

KAITLIN. Places for scene three!

JOHN. I'll get you for this.

OLI. Oh put a sock in it.

JOHN. I will. And then I'll get you.

> (JOHN, AMY, MORRIS, *and* DANIELLE *exit grumbling.* BILL *comes over.*)

> (KAITLIN *sets up a hospital bed.*)

BILL. Hey there boss man.

OLI. I don't have time, Bill.

BILL. I know, right? Who has time these days? Anyhoo, I've got a date tonight with a smoking hot—

OLI. No.

BILL. In fact, I have three dates—

OLI. No. You're not leaving.

BILL. Can I invite them to the set?

OLI. No. Go to your dressing room.

BILL. Man you used to be cool. Now...you disgust me.

> (BILL *walks off.*)

I'll remember this.

> (KAITLIN *sets up a hospital bed.*)

KAITLIN. Places in the hospital!

> (MONA JEFFRIES *[played by* CYBIL*] gets in to the bed.*)

OLI. And Five Four Three Two...

> (*Stirring soap opera music plays.*)

> (MONA *lies in bed, shaking her head back and forth in some kind of hallucinatory fever.*)

MONA. No...no...please... You can't do this to them...

> (*She shakes herself awake.*)

Oh. It was just a dream.

> (DOCTOR WILLIAM, *[played by* TYLER*] enters in a lab coat.*)

DOCTOR WILLIAM. I see you're feeling better Mona.

MONA. Doctor, I had the dream again.

DOCTOR WILLIAM. It's just a result of the sedative I gave you.

MONA. No it's not! They're in trouble! I know they are.

DOCTOR WILLIAM. *(Passionately overacting:)* You need to get a hold of yourself, Mona, there's a great big world out there that needs you, it needs your spirit, your energy, you can't let yourself be dragged down into the malaise of this swamp—I tell you to Get up and Live! Live like you've never lived before! And then all those people who doubted you—you're going to sign their death warrant—

OLI. CUT!

TYLER. What!

OLI. Stop adding lines! This isn't an audition for your movie!

TYLER. Did we get that take though? Can I have that for my reel?

OLI. No you cannot have that for your reel!

BROOKE. I already deleted it.

TYLER. Are you kidding me?!

OLI. Take it back and do it again!

KAITLIN. And Five Four Three Two

DOCTOR WILLIAM. *(Still overacting:)* You need to get a hold of yourself Mona.

MONA. I'm trying, Doctor, but the dream seemed so real. I have to warn my grandchildren.

DOCTOR WILLIAM. Shhhh. This will help you sleep.

MONA. No please! I need to get out of here!

DOCTOR WILLIAM. You need to sleep.

(He administers a drug and MONA falls asleep.)

You need to sleep for a long, long time.

(He smiles evilly. SEQUOIYA, a naïve hippy [played by LILY] enters.)

SEQUOIYA. William!

DOCTOR WILLIAM. Sequoiya! I thought I told you never to come to me here!

SEQUOIYA. I just needed to see you! They're saying such terrible things about you!

DOCTOR WILLIAM. No!

SEQUOIYA. Yes!

DOCTOR WILLIAM. No!

SEQUOIYA. It's not true, is it?

DOCTOR WILLIAM. Of course it's not true!

SEQUOIYA. You didn't give someone a hamster kidney instead of a real kidney in a bizarre transplant scam?

DOCTOR WILLIAM. Where would I even get a hamster kidney? I don't even think hamsters have kidneys.

SEQUOIYA. You didn't steal a hamster from a kindergarten class and use it in experiments? And then sold the real kidneys on the black market to Serbian gangsters who in turn financed an independent film about Dungeons and Dragons?

DOCTOR WILLIAM. Darling, darling, it's me. It's Doctor William. I would never harm a hamster. And I don't like independent film or Serbians.

SEQUOIYA. Oh I was so worried!

DOCTOR WILLIAM. Don't be. Remember—there's a great big world out there that needs you, it needs your spirit, your energy, you can't let yourself be dragged down into the malaise of this swamp—I tell you to Get up and Live! Live like you've never lived before! And then all—

OLI. CUT!

TYLER. Dang it! You have crossed me for the last time!

OLI. Go back!

KAITLIN. And Five four three two—

SEQUOIYA. Oh I was so worried!

DOCTOR WILLIAM. Don't be. Here—take some of these pills and you'll feel better.

SEQUOIYA. What do these do?

DOCTOR WILLIAM. DON'T QUESTION ME!

(He stops.)

I'm sorry. They'll calm you for a time. Take them now.

SEQUOIYA. Okay.

(She takes the pills.)

SEQUOIYA. I already feel better and am no longer concerned about your possible organ harvesting.

DOCTOR WILLIAM. Excellent. Now why don't you lie down over here? Oh—you look so lovely today—

SEQUOIYA. Thank you. Can I just sleep here?

DOCTOR WILLIAM. Sure. You can sleep for a long, long time.

(He smiles evilly.)

Oh nurse—I believe we have another candidate for a kidney transplant.

(He laughs evilly.)

OLI. I don't buy the laugh!

TYLER. Are you kidding me?!

LILY. That laugh was pathetic. It should be like

(She laughs evilly.)

BROOKE. Or more like

(She laughs evilly.)

CYBIL. My uncle laughed like that. He had an evil streak too—he owned a bear, and trained it to attack my sister-in-law because…at least I think he did. But his laugh—I remember it—

(She laughs evilly.)

No that wasn't it. More like

(She laughs evilly.)

KERI. How about this!

(She laughs evilly.)

OLI. How about

(He laughs evilly. Everyone else begins joining in with their own evil laugh.)

TYLER. Fine!

KAITLIN. Five Four Three Two

DOCTOR WILLIAM. Oh nurse—I believe we have another candidate for a kidney transplant.

(He laughs maniacally for a long, long time.)

OLI. No.

DOCTOR WILLIAM. Oh nurse—I believe we have another candidate for a kidney transplant.

(*He laughs moderately evilly.*)

OLI. And CUT.

TYLER. There.

OLI. We'll dub in the laughter later.

LILY. Can I do it?

OLI. Sure.

TYLER. You're a hack.

OLI. And you're a talentless poser, so there you go.

LILY. I agree with both of you.

OLI. Get off the set.

(TYLER *and* LILY *exit.*)

KAITLIN. Take Five.

BROOKE. Take Five.

(BROOKE *and* KAITLIN *exit.*)

KERI. What are we doing?

OLI. We're taking a break.

KERI. I love breaks! They're so restful!

OLI. You're really smart, you know that?

KERI. Ohmigosh do you mean that!? That's so awesome! So tell me everything you know! I want to be a director too someday! And a movie star! Like Ron Howard except with more hair!

OLI. Can you just leave me alone for a second so I can have my break?

KERI. Sure but just know that I'm going to learn everything I can possibly learn from you and then I'm going to become you—not in a creepy way I know that kind of sounds stalkerish but I'm not a stalker I'm just really, really enthusiastic—like I'm not gonna wear the same clothes as you but wouldn't it be fun if we did that for Halloween?! Like you could be the intern and I'd be the director and then we could fool all of our friends—

OLI. Leave me now freak girl!

KERI. Yes. Leaving now! Leaving. I'm going. Bye!

(*She leaves, then comes back.*)

KERI. I just wanted to say that I'm leaving.

(She leaves.)

Are you lonely?

OLI. No! Go away!

(She leaves again.)

(OLI sighs, then picks up a cell phone and dials.)

OLI. *(Into phone:)* Yeah I'm not going to make it home tonight, so you'll need to water the plants. They need it every day. I don't care if you're busy, I've got orchids—they are demanding—

(The lights go out.)

That's weird. Power just went out. It's an old building I guess.

(There's a loud Thump somewhere in the room.)

Hello? Hello? I gotta let you go.

(He hangs up the phone.)

Is there anyone in here?

(Someone attacks OLI in the darkness. We hear a loud WHUMP and OLI falls to the floor. The mysterious figure tries to dart away.)

OW! That really hurt! Why would you—

(The mysterious figure returns to finish the job. We hear WHUMP WHUMP WHUMP.)

OW! OW! OW!

(The mysterious figure runs around, pulls something off a table and hits OLI again. The figure waits for a second to make sure he's really dead, then darts off.)

(The lights come back up. OLI is lying dead on the floor.)

(Moments later, DANIELLE enters happily.)

DANIELLE. All right I'm ready for my next fight scene! I put on the long nails just like you said!

(She stops and looks around.)

Oli?

(She sees him on the ground.)

Gosh when you said take five you really meant take five.

(KAITLIN enters from the opposite side of the stage.)

KAITLIN. You ready Danielle?

DANIELLE. Psyched!

KAITLIN. All right let's get Bill out here. Bill! Scene Four! Places!

> (Re: OLI:)

What's he doing?

DANIELLE. Power nap.

KAITLIN. I wish I could do that.

> (BILL enters. He has lipstick on.)

Bill.

BILL. What?

KAITLIN. Who was it this time?

BILL. What are you talking about?

KAITLIN. Lipstick. Wipe it off.

BILL. I can't help it if I give off a certain animal magnetism. I also use musk ox spray. Awesome pheromones. You don't even realize you're going wild for me but you are.

KAITLIN. I'm not.

BILL. Your mind says no but your pheromone receptors say yes.

DANIELLE. *(Flirty:)* Hi Bill.

BILL. What's up babe?

DANIELLE. *(Flirty:)* You smell nice.

BILL. I know.

KAITLIN. Put your hormones in your pocket for a minute.

BILL. In my pocket?

KAITLIN. Oli are you ready? OLI. Wake up.

DANIELLE. Man can that guy sleep.

KAITLIN. Oli. OLI.

DANIELLE. Maybe somebody killed him.

KAITLIN. *(Examining* OLI:*)* Ah!!!! Somebody killed him!

BILL. *(Screaming like a little girl:)* EEEEEEEEEEE!

> (Everyone comes running. MORRIS and CYBIL come from the direction of their dressing rooms—KERI comes in holding a coffee—AMY enters in a huff. Moments later, TYLER enters, again on his cell phone, followed by LILY and JOHN. Finally, BROOKE saunters in.)

BILL. Oli's been murdered!

(DANIELLE slaps him.)

Ouch!

DANIELLE. Snap out of it!

BILL. I snapped out of it already!

DANIELLE. Oh. Sorry.

JOHN. Just what in the heck is going on here?

KAITLIN. Someone murdered Oli!

JOHN. Hmph. Bout time.

CYBIL. This is the last thing I needed today! The last thing! Wait what's happening?!

MORRIS. Murder.

CYBIL. *(Falling into character:)* Murder?! Here? I'll stop them! You won't make me talk!

MORRIS. We're not filming right now Cybil.

CYBIL. Oh. Oh this is real? Strange.

TYLER. *(Into the phone:)* I can totally play eighteen. Yeah. Absolutely. I've got a really young face and I know a great plastic surgeon who—hello? Hello?

(He looks around in shock and horror.)

I just lost my service.

AMY. I just lost my service!

TYLER. Everyone check your phones!

DANIELLE. Hey—

TYLER. *(Panicking:)* Check your phones!

(Everyone starts checking their phones. None of them have service.)

KERI. I can't even get my email!

TYLER. Help! Helllllp!

MORRIS. All right shut up! Can we focus for one second on the director that's been murdered!

JOHN. How do you know he was murdered, huh? Maybe he just choked to death on his own stupidity.

KERI. *(Helpful:)* Something could have fallen on him!

MORRIS. I can answer that. Some of you don't know this, but I had a cameo on *Law and Order*.

KERI. Oh thank heavens!

MORRIS. Let me examine the body.

(Everyone clears the way for him.)

This man...is dead. By unnatural causes. As a result of trauma.

DANIELLE. What do you think as a professional?

MORRIS. He's been murdered.

BILL. Aaaaah!

DANIELLE. Bill—

BILL. Please don't slap me again!

CYBIL. It's not all that gruesome. I've seen a lot worse murders in my day. I remember when our assistant producer was killed back in seventy-nine—cats. Drowned in cats. Darndest thing you ever saw. Sometimes I close my eyes and I can still see the furballs.

LILY. That was on the show, right?

CYBIL. No I think that was real.

LILY. Why would you kill someone with cats?

JOHN. Because they can't talk afterwards. Not that I know anything about that unfortunate event because I happen to have an alibi and I was cleared of all charges.

KERI. Do you think Oli was killed with cats?

MORRIS. No he was definitely not killed with cats! That's the stupidest way to kill someone ever!

JOHN. But effective. And they can't trace it. Not that I would know.

MORRIS. We have a situation here—Oli has been murdered—the doors are locked from the outside, I can only conclude...that one of you did it.

(KAITLIN grabs Oli's hat and puts it on her head.)

KAITLIN. And that is pretty terrible. Still, we have a production schedule to go through and an entire episode to shoot, so I suggest we film the rest of the episode and then talk about this.

AMY. WHAT?!

BILL. Who died and made you director?

KAITLIN. He did. I was the assistant director. Now I'm the director. And I say we move on from this sad event and pick up what's left of our lives.

MORRIS. He's still right here!

KAITLIN. And I expressed my condolences, but let's be fair, nobody really liked him and he wasn't getting great performances out of you guys, so he was expendable.

MORRIS. This is a murder investigation!

KAITLIN. No this is the set of a soap opera!

AMY. Wait a minute! Why are you in such a rush to get back to filming?

BILL. And so quick to take over!

TYLER. Maybe you killed him!

JOHN. Hmph. Just like a woman. Murderer.

KAITLIN. Whoah, hold on, that's ridiculous—

MORRIS. May I remind some of you that you threatened to kill him several minutes ago? John?

JOHN. So. I had good reason. Just so you all know: if I don't get soup, somebody dies. Not that I did it.

MORRIS. And Tyler?

TYLER. It was a line from a movie, you moron. You think you're so smart but you just signed your DEATH WARRANT.

MORRIS. Are you still rehearsing?

TYLER. No that was actually a real threat against you. Watch yourself.

DANIELLE. And I heard Bill threaten him later!

BILL. Oh come off it. If anyone's the killer here, it's Danielle.

DANIELLE. Me?

KERI. Yeah! It all makes sense! It was Danielle! She's the killer!

DANIELLE. I'm the nicest person here.

AMY. But how do we know it's not all an act?! You could have been acting this whole time! That's what you do for a living, right? You're an actor!

DANIELLE. We're all actors!

TYLER. You people are actors, I'm a star.

MORRIS. Where were you when he was killed?

DANIELLE. I was in my dressing room. Playing dress-up!

CYBIL. But you look behind you—who's that face in the mirror? A man, a strange man—

DANIELLE. No! I was alone! You can't think I would kill him! I don't have a motive!

LILY. Here's a motive for you! You're a washed-up has-been at age twenty-three and you've been in and out of acting camps every summer since you were twelve—secretly you're aware that you're not very talented and not as attractive as you think you are—you've got one chance left to prove yourself—to give the best acting performance of your life, so what do you do? You kill the director and act like you didn't kill him. If you can sell that, you can sell anything. Well, sweetheart, the Oscar for being a lying murderer is called prison, and that's where you're headed.

(*Stunned silence.*)

DANIELLE. You're saying I killed him for acting practice?

KERI. And to think I trusted you!

DANIELLE. I didn't kill him!

(LILY *starts a slow clap.*)

LILY. Bravo, Danielle. Bravo.

BILL. Danielle didn't kill him.

LILY. How do you know?

BILL. I was listening to her door the whole time.

AMY. I thought you were making out with me the whole time!

BILL. I was making out with you and listening to the door at the same time.

AMY. What?!

KERI. That's so romantic!

AMY. Why do I keep falling for you?

BILL. Because I'm a matador of love, baby. A matador of love. And you're the bull. Charge for the red flag. Whoops. It's gone. And I dance around you and wear tight pants at the same time.

AMY. We are so over.

BILL. So be it. But that means Bill is on the prowl, ladies.

LILY. I'll lock my door.

BILL. Your door says no, and your heart says probably not, but your feet say maybe.

KAITLIN. People. Can we focus for a second here? I know we're all concerned about who murdered Oli, but we have a deadline here. This episode has to be in the can by eight a.m. tomorrow or heads are gonna roll. More heads. And not in the literal sense.

MORRIS. Let's hope.

AMY. Look, I'm not going to go out there and act in a soap opera after the director has been killed—I can't do it—

KERI. I'll take her part!

AMY. All right fine I'll do it.

KERI. But seriously, if you need me for anything I'll do it. I'll even be the director!

KAITLIN. That's okay I've got the director's hat, that makes me the director, and that means I'm angry with all of you! Let's go to places for scene four!

MORRIS. Can I point out that we haven't even come close to discovering the killer?

KERI. Places for scene four! Ooh can I be the stage manager now?

KAITLIN. Knock yourself out. It's a thankless job and nobody likes you.

JOHN. True.

MORRIS. There is a dead body here.

KAITLIN. Stage manager's job!

KERI. Darn it! Can I get some help?

KAITLIN. Sweetheart, they're the talent. You're the stage manager. That means they don't help you, okay? You're going to have to drag off the body by yourself and find a place to store it, probably make arrangements to have it removed—and by the way you're not getting paid anything.

KERI. This is worse than being an intern!

(KERI *starts to drag his body off.*)

KAITLIN. Yep.

MORRIS. Guys?

TYLER. I'm not helping I just got a manicure.

MORRIS. No I mean don't you want to discover the killer?

CYBIL. Maybe you're the killer.

MORRIS. For the record, you're all a bunch of heartless sociopaths.

LILY. That's why my therapist said I'd be perfect for Soap Opera.

KAITLIN. We need Eileen and Jake!

KERI. Eileen and Jake!

KAITLIN. Everyone else off!

TYLER. I just hope no one would have the audacity to try to kill me when I'm off-stage.

(The rest of the cast exits as KERI returns.)

MORRIS. I don't really think that I can do this—

KAITLIN. I guess Soap Opera Digest was right—you have lost your mojo.

MORRIS. All right fine. But after we do this scene we work on who killed the director.

KAITLIN. I'm not making any promises. Places.

KERI. Places! And Five Four Three Two One—

BROOKE. You don't say one.

KERI. It comes after two.

BROOKE. I went to kindergarten too. You don't say one. You stop at two and make a silent one.

KERI. Why?

BROOKE. Just shut up and do it before I strangle you.

KAITLIN. Brooke. Try it again Keri.

KERI. Thank you so much for giving me another chance! Between you and me, you're so much better than Oli ever was. I really really think it's great that strong women are getting ahead in this business—like, my whole career, I want it to model right after you. Are you a size six? Cause I could totally wear those clothes. Oh Sorry! And Five Four Three Two—

(Lights up on JAKE STRONG [played by MORRIS] sitting on the couch in EILEEN's living room.)

(EILEEN enters.)

EILEEN. Jake Strong!

JAKE STRONG. Thought I'd find you here.

EILEEN. It's my house!

JAKE STRONG. That's why I thought I'd find you. How are you, Eileen?

EILEEN. You can't just walk back into my life like this!

JAKE STRONG. I can and I am. Doing it. Walking. You always liked the way I walked, didn't you?

EILEEN. Please leave. It's too painful to see you. Too painful!

(She starts to cry.)

JAKE STRONG. Is it any more painful than being massaged with porcupines? Because that's what I feel when I look at you. Look at me.

EILEEN. No.

JAKE STRONG. Look at me!

EILEEN. No!

JAKE STRONG. Look. At. Me.

(She looks. It's even more painful.)

EILEEN. Arrrghghg!

JAKE STRONG. You're still beautiful, Eileen.

EILEEN. Please Jake Strong. You're married. I was at your wedding in secret.

JAKE STRONG. I know. But there's something you never told me.

EILEEN. I told you my whole heart!

JAKE STRONG. I spoke with Valencio Di Carpathio today.

EILEEN. No!

JAKE STRONG. Yes! And you know what he told me about my darling wife? My wife that I loved constantly for the past one and half years after rescuing her from gypsies?!

EILEEN. I know.

JAKE STRONG. You couldn't tell me?!

EILEEN. How could I tell you? You wouldn't listen!

JAKE STRONG. She's the daughter of my arch-enemy! I can't even look at her now! Every time I look at her I see his evil face.

EILEEN. Just turn her around then.*

(*This line may be cut.)

JAKE STRONG. It's just so terrible!

EILEEN. She might be his daughter, but she might not be evil. You could give her a chance.

JAKE STRONG. No! It's over! My marriage is over!

> (*He turns to her.*)

EILEEN. What does that mean for us?

JAKE STRONG. Eileen.

EILEEN. Jake Strong.

JAKE STRONG. No! I can't do it! I can't do this!

EILEEN. I can't live knowing you're with another woman!

JAKE STRONG. You must!

EILEEN. I can't!

JAKE STRONG. You must! I shouldn't have come here. I can't see you. It's too painful.

> (*He looks at her and the pain is intense.*)

Aarrrhghg!

EILEEN. Your brother was here today.

JAKE STRONG. Gary?

EILEEN. No. Sebastian.

JAKE STRONG. Sebastian Strong is not my brother. He's a genetic experiment gone wrong.

EILEEN. My daughter is going to marry him.

JAKE STRONG. Nooooo! I'll kill him!

EILEEN. Don't try Jake! He's been trained by Navy Seals! And he also went to ninja school! You don't stand a chance.

JAKE STRONG. He must be stopped.

EILEEN. I know. But how?

> (*Pause.*)

KAITLIN. CUT! What are you waiting for?

AMY. There's supposed to be a doorbell there. Sequoiya comes in.

KAITLIN. Sequoiya you ready?

LILY. (*Off-stage:*) Mmmgh.

KAITLIN. Where's Keri?

MORRIS. Probably with Bill.

KAITLIN. *(Calling out:)* Bill I will murder you with my bare hands!

MORRIS. Maybe let's do something new today and not make any more death threats?

KAITLIN. Bill leave Keri alone!

AMY. *(Calling off:)* You are a sad pathetic man and I never loved you but if you change your mind I'm still available!

MORRIS. You know Amy I'm single.

AMY. That must be very nice for you.

KAITLIN. Let's keep going. And Five Four Three Two—

JAKE STRONG. He must be stopped.

EILEEN. I know. But how?

(Short pause.)

JAKE STRONG. I hear the doorbell.

EILEEN. I didn't hear it.

JAKE STRONG. I have amazing ears.

(JAKE STRONG strides to the door and opens it. LILY tumbles to the floor.)

KAITLIN. CUT! Lily this isn't time to fake one of your fainting spells for a party game again!

(LILY is lying there on the floor.)

AMY. She seems a little out of it.

(MORRIS leans down.)

MORRIS. She's dead! I'm sure of it!

KAITLIN. What the heck is going on around here?!

AMY. Well she was in poor health.

MORRIS. She wasn't in poor health, she was murdered!

AMY. You can be in poor health and be murdered at the same time. It happened to my Aunt. Get a life.

MORRIS. Someone killed her. Look.

(He takes a knife out of her back.)

This is a knife.

AMY. It was Morris!

MORRIS. I was standing in front of you when it happened!

AMY. It could have been a slow-acting knife.

MORRIS. There's no such thing as a slow-acting knife! There's a murderer loose backstage! Round everyone up!

KAITLIN. I hate to interrupt your little witch hunt, Morris, but I'm still the director here. And I make the decisions on whether or not we round everyone up so you can freak out and interrogate everyone.

MORRIS. There are two dead people now!

KAITLIN. Think about how many people die on this planet every day and you'll see what a ridiculous statement that was. Have a little perspective, please.

(*Other cast members are entering.* BILL *enters with* DANIELLE, *followed by* CYBIL *and* JOHN, *in the middle of an argument.*)

JOHN. (*Arguing:*) No that was in seventy-two! I remember I had gout, and you thought I said goat, and for some reason you loved goats—

CYBIL. I never loved goats you senile old codger!

JOHN. Your third husband was a goat—

MORRIS. People! Please. Where's Tyler?

(TYLER *enters, freaked out.*)

We have a crisis.

TYLER. I know that!

MORRIS. So—

TYLER. WHY ISN'T ANYONE DOING ANYTHING ABOUT THE CELL PHONE SERVICE?!

(AMY *slaps him.*)

AMY. That was fun.

MORRIS. Are we missing anyone?

(*They look around. After a second,* KERI *enters sunnily.*)

KERI. Hi!

MORRIS. Where were you?

KERI. I got lost! It's so amazing back there!

MORRIS. All right— We've had another murder.

CYBIL. Oh come on didn't we just do a murder? Do we have to use the same plots over and over again?

MORRIS. Someone killed Lily.

BILL. EEEEEEEEE!!!

AMY. Oh put on some pants Bill.

BILL. You'd like that, wouldn't you?

AMY. You are disgusting and sad and pathetic.

BILL. And yet…you are drawn to me, like a parking cop to a flashing parking meter.

AMY. …yes.

DANIELLE. Hey!

BILL. Sorry. I can't help myself.

MORRIS. Bill—cool it.

KAITLIN. Or someone's gonna kill you.

MORRIS. No no no—stop making threats! There are people getting killed!

TYLER. But she didn't even have a major role.

MORRIS. It doesn't matter!

TYLER. To you, maybe.

MORRIS. There is a murderer amongst us!

JOHN. Listen to college boy using a word like amongst.

MORRIS. This is like herding cats. Everyone sit.

(*Everyone sits.* AMY *and* DANIELLE *sit on either side of* BILL.)

JOHN. I want a cushiony chair.

MORRIS. JUST SIT DOWN!!

(JOHN *does.*)

We're locked in. Someone has cut our cell phone service—get a grip Tyler—Oli was bludgeoned to death, and now Lily has been stabbed. The killer is sitting right here.

KERI. This is exciting!

KAITLIN. And also we have to finish filming our episode—

MORRIS. No we don't! We can stop filming the episode because that's what any sane, decent human beings would do!

KAITLIN. Which is precisely why we'll continue to film the episode—the killer would expect us to stop, so we won't.

MORRIS. Have you been replaced by a robot or something? You used to be nice!

KAITLIN. That was before I assumed power. And now I've been corrupted.

KERI. That sounds great!

KAITLIN. You wouldn't believe.

DANIELLE. I'm up for anything, really. I could talk about the murderer or I could film another scene.

KAITLIN. That's a great attitude Danielle.

MORRIS. No it's not no it's not!

KAITLIN. Morris—If we allow the killers to change who we are and prevent us from filming this show, then they're already won.

MORRIS. No actually if they *kill people* and *get away with it* then they win!

JOHN. I know a thing or two about murder. And it's this: If a murderer wants to be caught, he'll be caught. If he doesn't want to be caught, you won't catch him. Especially if he's careful and uses a technique no one's thought of before. But I don't know anything about that.

BILL. I think John's right. No use going after the killer.

DANIELLE. Yep.

(Everyone ad libs in agreement except for MORRIS.)

KAITLIN. All right that's settled. Moving on. We need to film this scene, but Lily is dead.

KERI. I'll play her part! I already had her costume altered to fit me and I memorized all of her lines backstage!

DANIELLE. You are so enthusiastic!

KERI. So are you!

(They hug.)

KAITLIN. Great! Okay—places for Sequoiya's entrance. Nice work, Keri.

(MORRIS can't contain himself.)

MORRIS. Don't you find it slightly suspicious that she already has the part memorized?

KAITLIN. No. I don't. And I don't like those insinuations. Places!

(KAITLIN returns to her director's chair. AMY gets back in position. Everyone else leaves. MORRIS looks to BROOKE for help.)

BROOKE. Don't look at me, I'm just the cameraperson. And I don't like you.

(MORRIS *shakes his head and gets back to his spot.*)

KAITLIN. And Five Four Three Two—

(Lights up on the set.)

JAKE STRONG. He must be stopped.

EILEEN. I know. But how?

(The doorbell rings.)

It's the doorbell.

JAKE STRONG. I know.

(EILEEN *answers the door.* SEQUOIYA *[played by* KERI *now] is there. [*KERI *is absolutely confident and over-the-top as an actor.]*)

EILEEN. Sequoiya?

SEQUOIYA. You're probably wondering why I look different. It was Doctor William.

EILEEN. I don't trust him.

SEQUOIYA. Yes, but I changed my appearance for him because I thought he would like me better…this way.

(She strides into the room.)

EILEEN. What are you doing here?

SEQUOIYA. I have to tell you something. Something I've never told anyone. A secret.

JAKE STRONG. Maybe I should go.

SEQUOIYA. No! Stay. It concerns you too. Please. I feel just awful.

(She stands and gives an impassioned monologue that is most certainly not in the script.)

Sometimes, when I'm alone and staring at the moon, I think about what it would be like to be weightless, to float above the earth and see all the problems here on this planet like an alien would, in some strange, incomprehensible language, maybe that alien wouldn't even have ears they'd just have sort of holes in the sides of their head that they would also breathe through—but I would twirl, oh how I would twirl out there in space, a spinning star of my own, giving out light and life to my own universe—and then here on this planet I could see the—

JAKE STRONG. *(Trying to cut her off:)* That's nice but—

SEQUOIYA. *(Cutting him off:)* No don't you see, Jake Strong! Don't you see the world around us?! The dazzling, mad, insane little place we call Earth? Sometimes I wish I was an octopus so I would have eight arms and be able to do lots of things at the same time, and also have suckers cause those would be pretty cool too although I imagine you might get stuck against a wall.

EILEEN. Maybe you could tell us what's bothering you?

SEQUOIYA. Oh. Okay! Remember how when your baby was six months old I was your babysitter?

EILEEN. Yes.

SEQUOIYA. Well when I was babysitting I switched the baby with another baby I had in the back of my car and no one noticed.

EILEEN. What?

JAKE STRONG. Nooooo!

KAITLIN. CUT!

(KERI claps for herself.)

KERI. Yay! My first scene!

MORRIS. We're gonna cut all that stuff out, right?

KAITLIN. Keri. Maybe you could use some suspense when you tell them you switched babies on them. We want to have suspense there.

KERI. No offense, Kaitlin, but you don't know what you're talking about and that was the stupidest direction I've ever heard in my life.

AMY. Okay—how is it possible I didn't notice she switched the baby when it was six months old? Wouldn't I have, like, seen the baby beforehand?

KERI. It's not like you were a good mother.

AMY. All right but—

KAITLIN. Maybe you were hypnotized.

AMY. By who?

MORRIS. By whom.

AMY. Shut up.

KERI. We'll just say I did it! That was such a brilliant idea just now!

KAITLIN. All right let's take it back—

KERI. Before my impassioned monologue?

KAITLIN. After your impassioned monologue, and remember, suspense.

KERI. Doesn't help me.

KAITLIN. Try again. Places!

(They return to their places.)

And Five Four Three Two—

(Lights come up on the set again.)

EILEEN. Maybe you could tell us what's bothering you?

SEQUOIYA. Oh. Okay! Remember how when your baby was six months old…

(With suspense:)

I was your babysitter!

EILEEN. Yeah I remember that.

SEQUOIYA. It was a night almost like this, sick and dark with a hint of alien invasion in the air, the baby wouldn't stop crying—she wouldn't stop! She just…wouldn't stop!

(She starts to cry.)

EILEEN. It's okay.

SEQUOIYA. I tried everything I even tried poking her with a stick but that didn't work. So I took her out to my car…

(With suspense:)

I had a spare baby in the car! I always carried one just in case. And I…I…

(Breaking down again.)

JAKE STRONG. What did you do?

SEQUOIYA. I switched the babies!

EILEEN. That's impossible I would have noticed that—

SEQUOIYA. No! You didn't! Because…

(With suspense:)

I hypnotized you!

EILEEN. So—you're saying—the girl we believe is Jessica…isn't our daughter?

(SEQUOIYA nods.)

JAKE STRONG. Noooooo!

KAITLIN. CUT!

(Lights change.)

Hey that was all right. Keri—there was a lot more suspense in that.

KERI. Yeah I was just inspired you know? I had no idea where that idea came from!

KAITLIN. Maybe it was when I told you to have more suspense in it.

KERI. Who can say?

KAITLIN. All right—Brooke? What's next?

BROOKE. Well, let's see, that was scene four, so I'm guessing that the next scene will be scene five. I'm going out on a limb there, though.

KAITLIN. All right, scene five. Ooh we need the gun. Keri?

KERI. On it!

(She exits.)

MORRIS. Kaitlin—maybe sending Keri to go get the gun is not the smartest—

KAITLIN. You just can't move on with your life, can you?

AMY. Hey there. I'm looking at the script for my next scene—some of these lines are pretty stupid. Like this one: How are you? Who says that?

KAITLIN. No you cannot rewrite the script.

AMY. Are you kidding me?! ARE YOU KIDDING ME you snot-nosed twit! I will eat you for breakfast with a side of hash browns! I've been on this show for fifteen years I know a good line when—

(MORRIS tries to escort her away.)

MORRIS. Amy. Amy. Deep breaths.

AMY. I'm still not dating you Morris.

MORRIS. That's not what I'm—

AMY. *(To* KAITLIN:*)* This isn't finished! You hear me?! I am not done with you!

KAITLIN. Stuff a sock in it Amy! Stuff two socks in it!

MORRIS. Ladies—

(AMY storms off.)

BROOKE. I love your touch with the actors.

MORRIS. Kaitlin, we have to stop filming—

KAITLIN. You're really obsessing about this and it's beginning to worry me.

> *(Calling out:)*

Let's get Sebastian and Valencio out here! And can we do something about this lighting? It's way too clear. I'd love to have a few more fake guns around too! Is there any way we can put live bullets in any of them? Morris—I need you backstage in the dark away from everyone else. People! As much as possible I'd like you to be alone, in the dark, confused, with a fake weapon! Can we try that?!

MORRIS. What is the point of that?

KAITLIN. I want some real authentic fear in these scenes. Let's do it!

> *(The lights get dim.)*

Morris. Time for you to go be alone—here take this fake gun.

> *(She hands him a gun.)*

MORRIS. I don't want the gun.

KAITLIN. It might be real, I don't know, I haven't checked. Off-stage now.

MORRIS. This is crazy!

KAITLIN. Hey! We've got new leadership okay? Crazy is how I do things. Let's go!

> *(MORRIS exits, muttering. BROOKE and KAITLIN remain onstage alone.)*

Is there any way we can get some sound effects?

> *(Thunder BOOMS.)*

Nice.

BROOKE. That wasn't me.

KAITLIN. I don't care.

> *(Another BOOM of thunder, followed by a GUNSHOT. Off-stage DANIELLE screams.)*

Save it for the cameras Danielle!

> *(BILL bursts on to the stage, clutching his chest.)*

BILL. *(Dying:)* It was…

KAITLIN. It was what? Finish your sentence!

> *(BILL points off-stage as DANIELLE runs on stage.)*

BILL. It…was…

(He dies.)

(Everyone comes out on stage. A couple of them wave fake guns.)

KAITLIN. Bill? Are you acting?!

DANIELLE. He's been shot!

(Everyone puts their fake guns behind their backs.)

Aaaaaaaaah!

(Everyone looks at her.)

Well someone needs to scream now that Bill's dead.

KAITLIN. He's dead?

MORRIS. That's what happens when you get shot!

JOHN. I've been shot four times and I'm not dead.

CYBIL. And I even did it once. And I apologized for it. Wait. Was that on the show or in real life?

MORRIS. What's going on here is that three people have been murdered tonight!

DANIELLE. Is it three? I lost count.

KERI. *(Helpful:)* Oli, Lily, and Bill.

DANIELLE. Thanks!

AMY. There's something pinned to him. It's a note!

DANIELLE. Aaaaaaaaah!

AMY. It's a note.

DANIELLE. I thought you said something else.

AMY. What do you think I said?

MORRIS. Does it matter? Read it!

JOHN. Don't touch it that's evidence.

AMY. Fine—I'll just look at it.

(She gets close to the body.)

Dear cast members of *The Bold and the Young*— Tonight—

(She stops.)

TYLER. Tonight what?

AMY. That's all it says. Tonight—

KERI. Maybe there's something written on the back!
DANIELLE. Ooh that's a possibility!
>   (AMY *gingerly lifts the note and tries to read the back of it.*)

AMY. Tonight—I am going to kill you all.
>   (*Thunder BOOMS.*)

MORRIS. NOW can we try to figure out who the murderer is?!
>   (*Lights down.*)

End of Act I

ACT II

(Dramatic soap opera music.)

(BROOKE is still filming. KAITLIN is in the director's chair. Lights up on the set of the show. VALENCIO DI CARPATHIO [played by JOHN] is sitting on his lounge chair, sipping sherry. JESSICA [played by DANIELLE] enters, holding an umbrella.)

VALENCIO. Ah. I see you found your way here.

JESSICA. I held my nose the entire time, Valencio di Carpathio.

VALENCIO. Such venom. I enjoy your hostility. Would you care for some sherry?

JESSICA. Never!

VALENCIO. It's been aged twenty years. Just like you.

JESSICA. Okay then I'll have some.

VALENCIO. I'll have to see some I.D.

(He laughs evilly.)

JESSICA. You're so evil.

VALENCIO. Correct. But I believe we must all embrace our true nature, isn't that right, Amelia?

JESSICA. My name is Jessica!

VALENCIO. Of course it is. Of course it is.

(He smiles evilly again.)

Would you like to join me in a game of checkers?

JESSICA. Never!

VALENCIO. Are you sure? I find checkers to be soothing to the soul.

JESSICA. What did you bring me here for?

VALENCIO. Curious, are you? Curious like a monkey.

JESSICA. Don't you mean like a cat?

VALENCIO. I don't like cats.

JESSICA. You monster!

VALENCIO. Indeed. Indeed. If you do not want to play checkers, perhaps we could play the Wii. I have some excellent games I've stolen from the internet.

JESSICA. How dare you download free content from the internet?! Don't you know those people work for a living! All the time they slaved—

VALENCIO. Spare me your morality lesson. I will not be swayed by a child.

JESSICA. What made you so evil?

VALENCIO. Do you want to know? Sit. And I will explain it to you.

 (JESSICA *sits.*)

 (VALENCIO *stops and breaks character.*)

JOHN. Do I have to say this?

KAITLIN. CUT! What is the problem?

JOHN. I wouldn't use the new script to have my hamsters poop on.

DANIELLE. You have hamsters?!

KAITLIN. Well we had to make some quick changes to make this thing make sense—

JOHN. Quick changes don't involve a three-minute monologue by me.

DANIELLE. Oh please do it! I just love listening to you act for three minutes!

JOHN. Maybe you could try acting too, for a change.

DANIELLE. Okay!

CYBIL. I'm gonna tell you what I told my last ex-husband: Quit whining and just do it.*

 (*This line may be cut.*)

TYLER. Can I have a three minute monologue?

KAITLIN. No! Do the scene.

JOHN. Over my dead body!

KAITLIN. That can be arranged!

MORRIS. Maybe that's something we shouldn't be saying?

JOHN. Fine. I'll do it.

DANIELLE. Yay!

KAITLIN. Thank you. And Five Four Three Two

 (*Lights change back to the set.*)

VALENCIO. Do you want to know? Sit. And I will explain it to you.

(JESSICA *sits.*)

KAITLIN. Can you sit more dramatically please? Take it back!

VALENCIO. Do you know what to know? Sit. And I will explain it to you.

(JESSICA *sits very dramatically.*)

It began when I six. I was a little boy then. My family was poor, my father dressed us up like monkeys and made us dance in the streets. But on my sixth birthday he promised me something: he would take me to a place called the Magic Kingdom in Orlando, Floreeda. It sounded magical. Mostly because it had the word magic in its name. So we saved all of our coins, and I danced a little bit harder than ever before, and I made my squeaking noises more realistic than ever, and we saved, and we saved, and soon, we had enough money to begin our journey. On our travels my father made amusing sketches of tourists driving racecars and after only five months, we reached the magic land: Floreeda.

(*He takes a dramatic stroll.*)

Oh how it glorious it looked to me then. The spires of the blue castle, the robot figures of the hall of presidents, the giant chipmunk in a dress. I was in heaven. And that's when I saw him: An enormous rodent the size of my great uncle Supka, an animal so powerful he looked like a god from mythology—made flesh, with saucers for ears and a smile that could swallow the world—he looked right at me, and I was made anew. I followed him—I would have followed that rodent to the edge of the universe, but when he thought no one was looking…

(*Chokes up.*)

When no one was looking…He. Removed. His. Own. Head.

(*He can barely continue.*)

…His…Head! He was no god! He was a pimply-faced teenager! Right then and there, I dedicated my life to evil. Later that night, I gathered a small group of street urchins and we ambushed the rodent as he was returning to the castle—He was large, but clumsy, and we toppled him quickly, our tiny fists raining blows of rage upon his battered body—when he lost consciousness we tore off his head and held it aloft in triumph—my reign of terror had begun. I spent the next few days stealing purses from old ladies and used the profits to hire a gang of Albanian dock workers—we held Snow White captive for days before they gave in to our demands. Five hundred thousand U.S. Dollars and a plane ticket to Italy. I left my father there to draw sketches and dance his monkey dance. From there it was easy to become overlord of an international crime syndicate. All because of the rodent.

JESSICA. Wow.

VALENCIO. So you see, your pathetic little concerns are of no importance to me. You can either stand with me, or I will destroy you. Because I am evil.

JESSICA. I'll never join you.

VALENCIO. Certainly. You are disappointing. But let me tell you something else:

JESSICA. There's nothing you can tell me!

VALENCIO. Your fiancé, Sebastian Strong?

JESSICA. Leave him alone!

    (VALENCIO *laughs evilly.*)

VALENCIO. My darling, he has been working for me for years.

JESSICA. I don't believe it!

VALENCIO. And in fact, his name is not Sebastian Strong at all—it is Samantha Strong!

JESSICA. WHAT!

    (SAMANTHA STRONG, *wearing an eyepatch, [played by KERI] enters.*)

SAMANTHA STRONG. It's true, Jessica.

JESSICA. Sebastian, is that you?

SAMANTHA STRONG. Yes.

JESSICA. You look so different!

VALENCIO. The wonders of modern plastic surgery.

JESSICA. You're like three inches shorter!

VALENCIO. Special boots.

JESSICA. I don't believe it.

SAMANTHA STRONG. I lied to you, Jessica. I've been lying all along—about my true identity, my gender, hair color, and facial features—I've changed them all back to the way they used to be.

JESSICA. But I loved you!

SAMANTHA STRONG. Ha ha ha ha.

JESSICA. But why would you do that?!

SAMANTHA STRONG. You don't understand, do you, Jessica, what would make a woman dress up like a man and pretend to be a man for six years, wear an eye patch, star in numerous schemes, and almost marry two different women before settling on you? It's so obvious, really.

VALENCIO. Sherry?

SAMANTHA STRONG. Thank you, I'd love some.

VALENCIO. Jessica? Would you care for a drink now?

JESSICA. I think I would.

VALENCIO. Too bad you're not twenty-one! Ha!

(Laughs evilly.)

JESSICA. I guess I'll just have a coke then.

VALENCIO. I only have generic cola brand from the supermarket.

(Laughs evilly again.)

JESSICA. You monster!

SAMANTHA STRONG. Which brings us back to me, the person you used to know as Sebastian Strong. I have here my diary—look upon it!

JESSICA. No!

SAMANTHA STRONG. Look upon it!

JESSICA. No!

SAMANTHA STRONG. I'll read it for you then. "December 9th. Dear Diary: I know it's been a long time since I've written to you, but I've just had the most horriblest day. Like this guy was in Geometry class and he was like so hot but"—I'll skip forward—"some days I think it would be better if I disguised myself as a man and wreaked havoc on the universe and then at some dramatically intense point in the future revealed that I was really a woman all long". So there it is.

JESSICA. But—

SAMANTHA STRONG. You see, I felt alone and distant, like a traveler from a far-off land. Perhaps even from outer-space. A creature with many arms and many feelings and thoughts, of loneliness, and sadness, and the desire, above all, to be loved, and yet, on the surface, really, really disgusting with sores and strange tentacles and things. Oh and one more thing: I'm pregnant.*

*(*This can be replaced with "I'm your real mother.")*

JESSICA. Noooooo!

KAITLIN. CUT!

KERI. Yay that was my second scene ever!

DANIELLE. You were so good!

KERI. You were so good!

DANIELLE. I was like, are you kidding me, she is so good!

KERI. I was thinking the same thing about you! And you're so pretty!

DANIELLE. You're pretty too!

KERI. But you're super pretty—you're so pretty I wish I could be you—I'll follow you around and wear the same clothes and cut my hair the same way and then I'll be just like you! Except only one of us can live.

DANIELLE. Okay!

JOHN. Can someone please shoot both of these women?

AMY. Can I point out again that no one is going to buy that Sebastian Strong was Samantha Strong all along?

CYBIL. We did it in seventy-five, with Karl. Remember Karl? He quit to be a dermatologist and we had to replace him with that librarian who wandered in?

JOHN. She was amazing.

CYBIL. And who do I have to kill to get some water around here?

MORRIS. No one. No one's killing anyone!

CYBIL. Well where's my water! Am I gonna have to go milk a cow myself?

(Everyone looks at her.)

Like in the old days. When you wanted water you went out to a cow and milked it.

JOHN. That was an episode in sixty-nine you old bat! When I grew up we used a well!

CYBIL. Maybe in your fancy-pants high-rise you went to the well, in my village we went to the cow instead!

KERI. Here's some water, Cybil!

CYBIL. Thank you nameless intern.

KERI. I'm Keri!

CYBIL. Whatever.

KERI. I'm playing the part of Sequoiya and Samantha Strong.

KAITLIN. I hate to interrupt this lovely connection, but we've only got two more scenes and the whole episode is done!

TYLER. Good then we can go home. I haven't been able to check the internet for almost thirty minutes—who knows what could be going on out there? I'm frightened.

MORRIS. I know you're tired of hearing this, but—

(TYLER's *phone rings.*)

TYLER. My phone!

(*He leaps up and down and answers it.*)

Tyler Tripodo. Really? Really? No that's okay. No we're all fine. Thanks.

(*He hangs up.*)

MORRIS. Who was that?

TYLER. The police or something. Wanted to know about the screaming and gunshots.

MORRIS. And you didn't tell them *three people were murdered!?*

TYLER. Oh. Slipped my mind. I'll just call them back.

(*Checks his phone.*)

My service is out again! Oh no!

MORRIS. You know what? Enough of this!

(MORRIS *stands up.*)

TYLER. (*Standing up in front of him.*) You're right! I'm mad as heck and I'm not going to take this anymore! You can take away our phones but you can never take away...our FREEDOM!

(*The other actors applaud.*)

DANIELLE. That was amazing.

TYLER. Brooke?

BROOKE. What.

TYLER. Did you get that on camera?

BROOKE. No.

TYLER. (*Starting his speech again:*) You're right! I'm mad as heck and I'm not going to—

BROOKE. I'm not going to film you.

KAITLIN. But I am. Let's go to the next Doctor William scene.

MORRIS. Fine! Let's just film the show then! Who cares that there's a murderer on the loose!

KERI. Yay!

MORRIS. No not yay! I was being sarcastic!

KERI. And you're doing great at it.

KAITLIN. Morris. It seems like the murders have abated.

MORRIS. Excuse me?

KAITLIN. There was a time when it seemed like people were getting killed all the time, but that period has passed and now we're free to move on. Right?

MORRIS. *(Flabbergasted:)* I just—I—

KAITLIN. *(Deep:)* Remember—the show must go on.

(Brief pause.)

Places for scene seven! Back to the Hospital!

(DANIELLE approaches and lays a comforting hand on MORRIS' shoulder.)

DANIELLE. If you need to talk, I'm here for you. 'Kay? But I'm not interested in a relationship right now, just so we're clear about that. I'm trying to be single for a while.

(MORRIS tries to walk away from her.)

My last boyfriend was killed.

KAITLIN. We need Doctor William, Mona, and Sequoiya!

JOHN. If anyone needs me, they can go to hell.*

*(*Line can be changed to "If anyone needs me, they can stuff it.")*

(JOHN exits, grumbling.)

DANIELLE. *(Sunnily:)* I better go check on him.

(She exits.)

JOHN. *(Off:)* Leave me alone you vacant female!

MORRIS. Maybe we should all stick together in case—?

AMY. I'm gonna go be backstage alone with a variety of dangerous items.

(She starts to leave.)

What? Oh don't be a wuss.

(She exits.)

KAITLIN. Morris. Off-stage.

MORRIS. Can I just wait here?

KAITLIN. Off!

MORRIS. Fine.

(He exits.)

KAITLIN. Okay, Cybil, I want you to really be crazy in this scene.

CYBIL. What?

KAITLIN. Like crazy?

CYBIL. Like a cow?

KAITLIN. Yes. Sure. Just like a cow. Just keep doing what you're doing.

(CYBIL gets dressed in a hospital gown and messes up her hair to appear "Crazy.")

KAITLIN. And Five Four Three Two—

(Creepy soap opera music plays as lights come up on the hospital. MONA [played by CYBIL] bolts upright in bed.)

MONA. Oh no!

(She gets out of bed.)

It can't be true! It can't!

(She scrambles and examines a bottle of pills near her beside.)

What is this? What can this be? It's...drugs. It can't be!

(DOCTOR WILLIAM [played by TYLER] enters quickly.)

DOCTOR WILLIAM. You're up?

MONA. Yes I'm up you terrible man! You've been feeding me drugs this whole time!

DOCTOR WILLIAM. Well this is a hospital.

MONA. Don't touch me! Get your hands off me! You're an evil doctor!

DOCTOR WILLIAM. You found out my secret, old woman, but it won't save you now.

(He grabs her.)

MONA. Noooo! Help! Help!

(SEQUOIYA [played by KERI, still overacting] enters.).

SEQUOIYA. What's going on here?

DOCTOR WILLIAM. She's having a hallucinatory episode! You have to help me restrain her!

MONA. No! He's evil!

DOCTOR WILLIAM. She's hallucinating!

MONA. He's been drugging me! Please!

DOCTOR WILLIAM. Darling, you must choose between us. Do you believe the ramblings of a crazy old woman, or the words of your one, true love, who also happens to be a doctor and is wearing a doctor's lab coat? Choose correctly, or you could be signing your DEATH WARRANT.

SEQUOIYA. I'm so confused! Doctor William—I love you, and I completely changed my appearance and personality for you, but...

DOCTOR WILLIAM. And I love you too—in fact—

(He gets down on one knee.)

Will you marry me?

MONA. Help! Ack!

(MONA begins to feel ill.)

SEQUOIYA. I—I—I don't know what to say—

DOCTOR WILLIAM. Say yes.

SEQUOIYA. But you have to explain something to me first—

(She pulls up the side of her shirt.)

How did I get this strange scar on the side of my stomach? Did you harvest my kidneys?

MONA. Aaaackkck!

(MONA starts really getting into it now, thrashing about, choking.)

DOCTOR WILLIAM. Darling, I can explain about your kidneys. I can give you one back, don't worry.

SEQUOIYA. You stole my kidney!

DOCTOR WILLIAM. Only for a little while, and you don't need both of them—

(MONA collapses.)

Woman I'm trying to have a love scene here!

MONA. Garhrhhghg...

(MONA dies.)

DOCTOR WILLIAM. Cut!

> *(He breaks out of character.)*

You can't just pretend to die in the middle of the scene Cybil!

KERI. I thought it was really realistic though!

KAITLIN. Cybil that was totally the wrong time to do that. Cybil?

BROOKE. She's probably dead.

KAITLIN. Can you hear us?

TYLER. Stand back everyone! I'm playing a doctor!

> *(TYLER examines the body.)*

She's been poisoned.

KAITLIN. In real life or in the show?

KERI. She's such a good actor—

TYLER. Either that or she just died of old age. In which case it's quite a coincidence.

KERI. Wow.

> *(MORRIS bursts on to the stage.)*

MORRIS. There! You see! Someone else has been killed!

KAITLIN. How did you know she died?

MORRIS. I heard you say it! Everyone get out here!

> *(The other cast members enter.)*

JOHN. All right how many times do we have to go through this?

MORRIS. Everyone! There has been another murder!

DANIELLE. Aaaaaaaaaaaah!

AMY. Really, kid?

MORRIS. But I know who the killer is!

AMY. Hold on there, little taco, I'm running this show.

MORRIS. No actually I'm the only one who's—

> *(AMY takes out a badge.)*

AMY. Amy Millhouse. F. B. I. Read it and weep.

KAITLIN. You're an FBI agent?

DANIELLE. That is so cool!

KERI. I want to be an FBI agent!

AMY. Sorry we don't let chicks in.

JOHN. Good.

MORRIS. No, I'm sorry, you are not an FBI agent, you've been on this show for fifteen years.

AMY. Deep undercover.

MORRIS. For what reason?

TYLER. This is awesome—I made out with an FBI agent.

AMY. What you don't realize is that the FBI has a lot of secret agents. A lot. Close to two million. In most every situation a crowd gathers, one of you is a secret informant sending vital information back to the government. I don't care where you are: pre-school, church, a theatre attending a show—several of the people around you are undercover government agents recording and transmitting your every word, thought, and deed. Why? Because your government loves you.

MORRIS. This is insane!

AMY. Insane? Or all too sane?

DANIELLE. *(Raising hand:)* All too sane!

AMY. That's right. My job is to solve these murders.

MORRIS. So where were you say, while the last three people were being killed?

AMY. My job is to solve murders, not stop them. If I would have stopped the murders I wouldn't have any murders to solve, now would I? Then I wouldn't be doing my job. That's how the government works—efficiency, efficiency, efficiency.

KAITLIN. I am so blown away by this.

AMY. So let's all have a seat and bring the criminal to justice.

(Everyone sits obediently except for MORRIS.*)*

KAITLIN. Sounds good.

JOHN. Finally some justice around here.

TYLER. At least someone is doing something.

KERI. I'm excited!

MORRIS. Excuse me?! EXCUSE ME?! NOW YOU SIT?! NOW YOU LISTEN?! I'VE BEEN TRYING TO CONVINCE YOU PEOPLE THAT THERE'S A KILLER ON THE LOOSE FOR AN HOUR! THREE MORE PEOPLE ARE DEAD!

KAITLIN. But we shot some great scenes.

MORRIS. How do you know she's FBI?! Maybe she's the killer!

DANIELLE. She's got that little badge thing. It says FBI on it. That's how you know.

MORRIS. It could be fake!

DANIELLE. Um...hello? FBI agents don't lie. It's in their rules.

MORRIS. All right genius, who's the killer?

AMY. Not so fast, Morris. There's an order to this. We have three murders.

MORRIS. Four.

AMY. I thought there were three. Oli. Bill. Cybil.

MORRIS. You forgot Lily.

KAITLIN. Would you just let her do her job?!

AMY. Okay—four murders. The question is: were they all killed by the same person, or do we have four separate murderers?

(Short pause.)

Or two murderers who killed one person each and one who killed two?

DANIELLE. I never thought of it that way.

KERI. This is like scrabble!

JOHN. You and your fancy pants technology.

AMY. Or one murderer who killed three people and two murderers who teamed up to kill a fourth person?

MORRIS. I know who the killer is!

AMY. No you don't!

MORRIS. Yes I do! It was Keri!

(Gasps from everyone.)

KAITLIN. Oh come on! Keri?!

MORRIS. Think about it! How many people got murdered in the thirty years before she got here? None!

JOHN. Not exactly true.

MORRIS. How many people in the nine hours since she got here? Four!

KAITLIN. Oh come on Keri wouldn't hurt a fly!

(BLAM! KERI smashes a fly.)

TYLER. You just hate women, don't you? You just can't stand women. Because you have saggy buttocks.

MORRIS. No—guys—listen—

AMY. I'm running this show—sit down—

MORRIS. Keri handed Cybil the water—she had a gun backstage when Bill was killed—she's already memorized everyone's part, she's taking everyone's place—does anyone else find it strange that she already had her own eye patch for goodness sakes?! She's the murderer! It's so obvious it makes my brain hurt! Just confess it Keri! Confess that you are a cold-blooded killer!

(Pause. Everyone looks at KERI.)

KERI. Nope.

(Everyone sighs in relief.)

AMY. Well that's good enough for me.

DANIELLE. What a relief!

TYLER. And you thought she was a killer.

JOHN. She really had me going there for a second.

AMY. I'm afraid your wild accusations have no merit, Morris. Keri is clearly not the killer, because that would be too obvious. So sit down, buckle your seatbelt, and get ready for a ride on the truth express. It's gonna hurt. If you're a killer.

MORRIS. There's just—there's just—

AMY. No I'm afraid our killer is much sneakier than that, which is why it might be...

(Dramatic flourish:)

Danielle!

KERI. I knew it!

DANIELLE. You already accused me once!

MORRIS. She has an alibi! Bill vouched for her!

AMY. And where is Bill now? Coincidence? We've already established your motive for wanting Oli dead. Acting practice. Now why would you want Lily dead?

KERI. *(Raising hand:)* Ooh! I know! I know!

AMY. *(Like a teacher:)* Keri.

KERI. Lily had to die because she was standing in the way of her getting on the show. With Lily out of the way she could take her part and then weasel her way into the cast!

(Short pause.)

MORRIS. No that's *your* reason for wanting her dead.

KERI. Oh. Then I don't know then.

JOHN. Allow me to shed some light on this. I think I understand female psychology better than anyone here. You see—when two youngish attractive females are placed within a cage, they inevitably begin a struggle to the death to compete for the attention of the dominant male, which in this case would be me. Most of the time this battle surfaces in snide looks, comments about clothing bought at the Gap, and the occasional devastating text message, and also knives.

DANIELLE. No I liked Lily even though she was cruel and terrible to me! She was my friend!

JOHN. Which is why she had to die.

AMY. John's theory makes a lot of sense—I think we know why she wanted to kill Bill. He had spurned her attentions and begun to flirt with other women on the cast—

MORRIS. No that's *your* reason to kill Bill.

AMY. Sorry I'm out of practice at this whole secret agent thing.

DANIELLE. I can answer this one. I did want Bill dead.

KERI. You monster!

DANIELLE. You ever really like someone a lot?

KERI. I like most people!

DANIELLE. Right, and I like most people, and I'm a great person on the outside. And really, to be fair, I thought Bill was a tremendous actor and just a really gentle soul—

AMY. He wasn't gentle all the time—

DANIELLE. And he'd talk about how much he enjoyed watching sunsets and walking on beaches and making out and everything—and that sure was nice, but…I hated him with the white-hot intensity of a thousand suns. I mean I really wanted to kill him. In horrible, horrible ways—I had dreams about, making a pool of acid and dipping him into it extremely slowly while he begged for forgiveness, and then his toes would melt and he would scream and his screams would sound like angels singing in my mind and then I would—

(She snaps out of it.)

DANIELLE. But I didn't kill him I just wanted to kill him every second of every day!

KAITLIN. So why were you dating him?

DANIELLE. I have a hard time saying no to guys.

MORRIS. So there's one question I have, Danielle—

DANIELLE. I am not interested Morris. We're just friends okay?

MORRIS. I wasn't asking you out on a date!

DANIELLE. I just feel how I feel.

AMY. Which brings us to Cybil, which if you ask me, was just overkill. She was old, why would anyone want to kill her?

JOHN. Cause she was an evil old witch.

AMY. Quiet, John.

KAITLIN. I think I understand it. If she killed Oli to practice her acting, what if she killed Cybil…to practice her acting some more?

(A hushed gasp from KERI, TYLER, *and* AMY.*)*

KERI. It all makes sense!

MORRIS. You're saying she killed two people, not one, but two, just to prove she could act like she didn't kill two people?

AMY. It's all so simple! If acting innocent after killing one person was difficult, acting innocent after killing two people would be even more difficult! You're going away for a long time, Sunshine, to a place without much sunshine except for the few hours you're allowed to walk the yard. Confess!

DANIELLE. I didn't do it! Please, doesn't someone believe me!

MORRIS. I believe you!

DANIELLE. Thanks Morris but I know you're just saying that because you're interested in more of a relationship than I can give you—

MORRIS. Danielle didn't kill anyone! Think about it! She's not that good of an actress!

(AMY considers this.)

AMY. I see your point.

DANIELLE. That's hurtful, Morris.

AMY. So if it wasn't Danielle, that focuses the lens of justice on…

(She spins.)

MORRIS. Keri.

AMY. Shhh! I'm focusing.

(She rotates slowly.)

MORRIS. How about Keri since she's the killer?

AMY. On...Brooke!

BROOKE. *(Not impressed:)* I didn't do it because I was out here the whole time, I had no motive, and I don't care about you people enough to bother with murdering you. Although I will add that today's killings have in no way perturbed me.

AMY. Okay it wasn't Brooke. That means it was most likely...John!

JOHN. What!

AMY. The old man!

JOHN. This is preposterous!

AMY. We all heard you threaten Oli with death over a cup of soup—

JOHN. I stand by those comments.

AMY. Which leads me to the conclusion that you are a man who enjoys his soup, which leads me to another conclusion that you enjoy the comforts of warm food, which leads me inevitably to my final conclusion that you killed Oli.

JOHN. That's some fancy reasoning for the FBI.

AMY. I learned from the best: the internet.

JOHN. I don't even know what that is!

AMY. But it wasn't enough to kill the director because he wouldn't let you have soup, was it? Oh no, that wouldn't stop your murderous rage, would it, old-timer?

JOHN. Blast you and your rhetorical questions!

AMY. Next on the list was Bill—

JOHN. Lily.

AMY. It was Lily?

JOHN. Lily was second.

AMY. Really? How do I keep missing that?

MORRIS. Because you're a terrible, stupid human being!

KERI. I like him!

AMY. So it was Lily. Why kill Lily? Oh sure there are the obvious reasons: she was annoying, she had questionable grooming habits— she was a mouth-breather, but that wasn't it, was it, John? No...that wasn't it at all.

JOHN. What are you getting at?

AMY. You killed Lily because...

    (Dramatic pause.)

She took your parking spot!

JOHN. How did you know about that?!

AMY. F.B.I. John. Federal Bureau of Investigation. That means I know stuff. You had the prime parking spot on the lot, a parking spot you had kept since 1973 when you stole it from Cybil—

KERI. No!

AMY. Yes! You think we wouldn't find that out? You held that spot for decades—under the big tree, close to the ramp, it was the perfect spot for a crotchety old man because not only was it close, but it provided you a view of the basketball court across the street so you could make grumbling comments about the youth of today—

JOHN. I hate those youth of today.

AMY. Exactly! But the good times couldn't last, could they John, because onto the set came a person who got up even earlier than an old man! A person named...

    (Dramatic pause.)

Lily!

    (Shocked gasps from DANIELLE and KERI.)

She was crazy, so she never slept, so she got here at 6:00 a.m. which was a full fifteen minutes before you arrived—and she took your precious parking spot. And in fact I overheard a confrontation you had with her only three days ago! I will now choose actors to recreate that conversation.

KERI. Ooh can I be John!

DANIELLE. I'll be Lily!

    (KERI and DANIELLE switch into re-creation mode. KERI gets crotchety.)

KERI. I couldn't help noticing young lady that you have taken my parking spot. And as I am a kind elderly man I would appreciate it—

DANIELLE. *(With unnecessary British accent:)* Buzz off wanker! I'll park wherever I want and no one can stop me! NO ONE! Ha ha ha ha!

KERI. Why you whippersnapper— Someday soon I'm going to take a knife and stab you in the back with it.

DANIELLE. You try it!

KERI. And scene.

(They bow.)

BROOKE. That was spectacular.

AMY. Motive established. Set and match.

MORRIS. There's still two more murders.

AMY. I'm getting to it! Bill you killed because he took two muffins at breakfast when we were clearly allotted one, and you took out Cybil because you were just plain cranky and needed attention.

(JOHN claps slowly.)

JOHN. Bravo, agent Amy. Bravo. An excellent performance. Unfortunately: bunk. Did I want to kill Oli? Yes. Did I want to kill Lily because she stole my parking spot? Of course. Did I want to see Bill die because he took two muffins when we're only supposed to get one? Who wouldn't? And did I want to kill Cybil because I'm generally a cantankerous old coot who doesn't like anybody—Yes. You're forgetting one thing, though: I'm also lazy. And to kill that many people takes a lot of work. Besides, with the four of them dead I don't have as much to complain about, so that makes me unhappy. And crankier still. So, would I have liked to go on a killing spree? Sure. Did I do it? Nope. I'd rather eat soup.

AMY. Dang it! Well that means the only logical murderer is...

MORRIS. Keri.

AMY. Tyler!

TYLER. I'm sorry?

AMY. Tyler!

TYLER. Sorry I haven't been paying attention. The internet came back on so I've been googling myself. I also have a Twitter feed to attend to. See?

(KERI gets a message on her phone.)

KERI. Ooh! "Bored, why doesn't anyone notice me? Can't wait to get out of TV." That's funny!

TYLER. You follow me on Twitter?

KERI. Yeah!

JOHN. What the heck are you people talking about? Twitter?

AMY. It's a new technology that's completely entranced everyone and will be gone within three years.

JOHN. Hmph.

TYLER. But please go ahead—I'm sorry I haven't been following this closely.

AMY. To recap, there are three people dead—

MORRIS. Four—

AMY. Four people dead, I'm a secret FBI agent, John, Danielle, Keri, and Brooke have been cleared, and you're the only logical suspect left.

TYLER. Except for yourself and Morris.

MORRIS. I don't think I'm a suspect here, actually.

TYLER. Oh really! Oh really?!

(He sets up his phone to record himself as he begins to cross-examine MORRIS.*)*

Allow me to present a picture of a man to the jury. A picture of a man so obsessed with the truth, that he would kill for it. A man... named Morris Nyborg. This man right here!

MORRIS. I was actually on camera during one of the murders.

TYLER. That's awfully convenient, isn't it? Too convenient. Let's examine this man for a moment, shall we? A man playing the part of Jake Strong, the romantic, dashing soap opera hero. A soap opera hero who did not make Soap Opera Digest's list of the ten hunkiest daytime stars! A soap opera hero so insecure that he would sew padding into the backside of his pants in order to make his buttocks more shapely! A soap opera hero desperately, madly in love with the woman who played his daughter on the show, Danielle Farris!

DANIELLE. That's me!

MORRIS. Why does everyone think I'm in love with her?

DANIELLE. You're in love with me? Oh Morris—I don't feel the same way about you.

MORRIS. I KNOW THAT!

TYLER. *(Continuing:)* A man also in love with the woman who played his ex-wife on the show, Amy White!

MORRIS. How can I be desperately in love with two women at the same time!

TYLER. How indeed? How indeed. Pathetic, isn't it, Ladies and Gentlemen? Truly pathetic. So what does this aging, not terribly hunky daytime star do to win the love of the women who played mother and daughter, which is sick by the way, he sets out to prove his manhood. Prove it the only way he knows how: By killing people. In his own mind, in the twisted logic used by those who are desperate for attention and shapely rear ends, only through brutal, vicious killing can a man be a man. Think of hunters. Or the NRA. Unfortunately, the ladies didn't come around, did they Morris? After Oli you figured one of them would fall into your arms, but you didn't count on Bill—

DANIELLE. He was dreamy.

AMY. We used to call him, El Matador.

TYLER. So you dispatched him with a gunshot—and through an ingenious ninjitsu technique known as "slow knife" you killed Lily while you were on camera. Amazing, isn't it?

MORRIS. Slow knife? What is slow knife?

TYLER. Shall I show you? Watch carefully everyone. I shall appear to do nothing, but in fact, slow knife will be occurring. Brooke, when I tell you to, duck.

BROOKE. Why?

TYLER. Because the slow knife is coming.

BROOKE. Why not just hit the door or something?

TYLER. It's more dramatic this way. Now: Slow Knife.

(TYLER *bows his head.*)

(*Pause.*)

(*Pause.*)

(*Pause.*)

Duck!

(BROOKE *ducks and* TYLER *drops a knife on the ground.*)

MORRIS. You just dropped a knife on the ground! That wasn't Slow Knife!

TYLER. Because I am not a ninja! But only a ninja would know that I had not executed Slow Knife properly! Therefore: Ladies and Gentlemen: The Killer.

DANIELLE. Morris—even though you've killed four people, I still don't find you attractive. I'm sorry.

AMY. I'm seeing a little more appeal in you, but still not enough.

MORRIS. I am not the killer! There's no such thing as Slow Knife—

KERI. But only a ninja would know that there was no such thing as Slow Knife!

AMY. Makes sense to me. Book 'em.

MORRIS. What? No.

TYLER. Think about it: Who's been the one pressuring us to discover the killer all along? Morris. Why would he do that? To deflect attention away from himself. Bingo.

MORRIS. All right let's paint another picture, shall we? A picture of Tyler Tripodo.

DANIELLE. Do we have paints?

MORRIS. A man who would do anything for fame, even kill for it.

TYLER. You say that like it's a bad thing.

MORRIS. The show's ratings are down, he's up for a big movie—

TYLER. With Matt Damon—

KERI. I love him!

MORRIS. But he might not get that part, so what does he do? He stirs up a scandal to increase his profile so that casting him would be viewed as a publicity stunt. How to create that scandal? Murder. First Oli, then his co-stars. If you couldn't be a big star on this show then you'd make sure that the show was big enough to launch the rest of your career!

TYLER. I was on camera when Cybil was killed!

MORRIS. And I was on camera when Lily was killed!

DANIELLE. He explained that: Slow knife.

MORRIS. And there's no such thing as slow poison?

DANIELLE. That would be ridiculous.

TYLER. Not only did I not kill Cybil, there's certainly no way I could have killed Bill: I can't shoot a gun.

MORRIS. Oh come on.

TYLER. No, seriously, does anyone have a gun I could borrow?

KERI. Oh here!

(KERI *produces the gun and hands it to* TYLER.)

TYLER. Look!

(TYLER *fumbles with the gun. Everyone ducks except for* JOHN.)

I'm wildly incompetent with this thing! It could go off at any time!

(*He swings around again, everyone ducks a second time.*)

KAITLIN. Put it down!

TYLER. I can't even manage that!

(*He swings around a third time, everyone ducks again.*)

KERI. Wheeee!

TYLER. Aaaah!

(*He drops the gun.*)

See? I couldn't have shot Bill.

JOHN. Pansy.

(AMY *grabs the gun.*)

AMY. All right now I've got the gun! Everybody put your hands in the air!

(EVERYONE *puts their hands in the air.*)

KAITLIN. So you're the killer?

AMY. No, I'm the FBI agent. I'm just going to use this gun to threaten someone into confessing.

MORRIS. Are you sure this doesn't violate any laws or anything?

AMY. Um…Hello? FBI. Laws don't apply to me.

DANIELLE. She's right!

AMY. Now—There's one more piece of evidence we haven't considered.

MORRIS. How about the murder weapon which you have in your hand which Keri handed to you? Does that possibly make you suspicious?!

AMY. I'm not referring to the gun—I'm referring to the note. This note!

(*She reaches into her pocket.*)

Where's the note?

DANIELLE. I think it's still pinned to Bill's corpse.

AMY. Hold on. Keri can you go get the note?

KERI. Sure thing!

MORRIS. You're sending Keri to go get it?! Are you insane?!

KERI. It's okay it's in my job description.

(KERI *scampers off.*)

MORRIS. Amy, listen to me. A four-year-old child could figure this out.

JOHN. Nonsense. Four-year-olds don't know anything.

MORRIS. It's Keri. Keri is the murderer. She had the gun. When she comes back, you need to—

(KERI *comes back in.*)

KERI. And I'm back! Miss me? Here's the note.

(*She hands it to* AMY.)

AMY. Now the note says, "Dear Cast Members of The Bold and the Young— Tonight"

(*She flips it over.*)

"I will kill you all."

DANIELLE. Aaaaaaah!

AMY. What we have here is the killer's handwriting. Evidence. Now—examining the text I find something suspicious about the "I" in tonight. It's dotted…with a heart!

KERI. I do that!

(MORRIS *can barely contain himself.*)

DANIELLE. I do that too!

JOHN. Me too.

(TYLER *sheepishly raises his hand.*)

TYLER. Guilty as charged.

(*Short pause.*)

Of the "I" heart thing. Not the murders.

AMY. Okay, so that's inconclusive.

KAITLIN. I guess we'll just have to film the final scene of the episode then.

MORRIS. Are you kidding me?! No! I know who the killer is!

AMY. Well speak up, I'm all ears.

MORRIS. I know that you all have the intellect of slow gerbils, so I will try to be as simple as I can about this. Only one person here had the motive and the opportunity to kill all four people.

KERI. Really?

MORRIS. Yes. Really.

KERI. Wow.

MORRIS. She has killed through a variety of means, but for the same reason: She wants more than anything to take our places. She's the worst stalker any of us have ever had: It's—

(BROOKE *clutches her back and screams.*)

BROOKE. Ack!

(*She topples over, a knife protruding from her back.*)

DANIELLE. Slow Knife! It was Slow Knife!

TYLER. Wow!

AMY. Morris Nyborg, you're under the arrest for the murders of Oli, Bill, Cybil, Brooke, and…

DANIELLE. Lily.

AMY. Thank you.

BROOKE. (*Getting up slowly:*) That really hurt.

AMY. Oh Brooke's not dead.

TYLER. Are you all right?

BROOKE. Yeah, I wear a lot of padded clothing. Just barely grazed me.

MORRIS. But who stabbed you? It wasn't Keri—

KERI. I was over here!

BROOKE. It was—

(*Gunshot.* BROOKE *keels over.*)

JOHN. Okay stop trying to kill Brooke!

TYLER. Hold on everyone. I'm still wearing my doctor's coat.

(*He examines* BROOKE.)

BROOKE. Ow. Man.

MORRIS. So if none of us is the killer then it has to be…

(MILES *enters.*)

MILES. Me.

KAITLIN. The evil producer!

DANIELLE. Hi!

AMY. Miles. You're the killer?

MILES. Yep!

KERI. But why?

TYLER. *(Looking at his phone:)* Wow you should see how much we're trending up on Google right now! Apparently there's all kinds of buzz over the five people who just got killed. Woo hoo! We're hot, baby! We're hot!

JOHN. All right!

MILES. What better way to increase our ratings than to create a disastrous spectacle of murder and intrigue? It's perfect. When a star dies on a television show, ratings go through the roof. When four stars and the director die, you're talking a ratings tsunami. So the good news for the survivors is: The show won't be canceled.

DANIELLE. Woo hoo!

JOHN. Yeah!

KERI. Finally a happy ending!

MORRIS. But this is insane!

AMY. Oh God you're not starting this again are you?

MORRIS. You'll never get away with this!

MILES. I know you're thinking, how can he possibly get away with this?

DANIELLE. That's not what I was thinking, but close.

MILES. Well—I said four stars were killed. So far there are three deaths. The fourth star to die, of course, is the murderer, and is so consumed with guilt that he…or she committed suicide afterwards. All the rest of us are free to go on with their lives.

KAITLIN. I'm listening.

MILES. Here's the deal: If you don't say anything, you can remain on the hottest soap opera on television—salaries go up, stardom for all, possible movie deals, if you keep your mouth shut. If you think you need to tell the truth about things, well…you become the killer.

DANIELLE. Quick question: What if everyone takes the deal?

MILES. Then Cybil was the killer and she felt so bad about it she poisoned herself.

KERI. That makes sense.

MILES. Well, everyone?

TYLER. I'll take the deal.

DANIELLE. Hey, I'm up for anything.

KERI. Yay!

JOHN. Hmph.

MILES. Is that a yes or no, John?

JOHN. A yes I guess.

KAITLIN. Hey, I'm just happy to be the director.

(MILES *turns to* AMY *and* MORRIS.)

JOHN. Amy? Morris?

AMY. Well, while working for the FBI I've discovered that I have a certain moral flexibility. So I guess this one of the things I can stomach for the greater good.

JOHN. It's just you, Morris. What do you say? Wanna be on a hit show?

MORRIS. I have very serious ethical reservations about this.

JOHN. Oh be a man.

KERI. Can I be Jake Strong?

MILES. Keri—please. We've got some understudies ready. Well Morris?

MORRIS. I'm afraid I'm going to have to decline your offer, Miles. You can try and kill me if you want—

MILES. Oh I'll do more than try, I'll—

(*He clutches his back. A knife is sticking out of it.*)

Aaaaaah!

(MILES *dies.*)

TYLER. Slow Knife.

MORRIS. But I didn't—I didn't do anything!

KERI. Oh that one was me. I interned for some ninjas before this.

DANIELLE. That's awesome!

TYLER. *(From a distance:)* He's dead.

JOHN. How do you know that?

TYLER. I can just tell.

AMY. Well that's that—everything's all wrapped up.

MORRIS. But I guess we'll have to take Keri to the police now.

AMY. Uh—no—I don't think so.

KERI. *(Happily:)* I'm the producer of the show now!

MORRIS. But—

AMY. Morris—I think you owe Keri an apology.

MORRIS. All right—Keri—I'm sorry I thought that all the evidence pointed to you being a killer. Now I know that you only killed one person, so you're all right in my book.

KERI. I'm still not going to date you, Morris.

DANIELLE. Right on!

BROOKE. You know I could probably use some medical attention seeing as how I've been stabbed and shot.

TYLER. You look fine to me.

KAITLIN. All right people! Let's film the final scene!

DANIELLE. Yay!

BROOKE. I'm really not feeling well over here.

JOHN. Man up, Brooke.

KAITLIN. Places for the final scene! We need Jake, Samantha, and Valencio!

(Lights change to Valencio's house.)

KAITLIN. And Five Four Three Two—

(Dramatic soap opera music plays as the lights come up.)

(VALENCIO and SAMANTHA STRONG are playing checkers.)

VALENCIO. King me.

(He laughs evilly.)

Oh I think our plan is working out quite nicely, don't you…Tabitha?

SAMANTHA STRONG. Don't call me that. I'm Samantha Strong, remember?

VALENCIO. Of course. Of course. King me again.

(JAKE STRONG *bursts in to the house with a gun.*)

JAKE STRONG. I'll kill you Valencio Di Carpathio!

VALENCIO. Ah, Jake Strong. As expected.

(SAMANTHA *plays checkers.*)

Allow me to present to you…Samantha Strong.

(*She stands up, with eye patch.*)

SAMANTHA STRONG. Nice to see you again, Jake Strong.

JAKE STRONG. Is this some kind of sick joke?

VALENCIO. I never joke. Never.

SAMANTHA STRONG. I do though. Knock knock.

JAKE STRONG. (*With intensity:*) Who's there?

SAMANTHA STRONG. Half-sister.

JAKE STRONG. (*With even more intensity:*) Half-sister who?

SAMANTHA STRONG. Half-sister who was once your half-brother.

JAKE STRONG. Noooo!

SAMANTHA STRONG. That's right!

JAKE STRONG. It can't be.

VALENCIO. That's because it isn't!

SAMANTHA STRONG. What?

JAKE STRONG. What?

VALENCIO. My dear Samantha, or should I say, Sebastian, you never were Jake Strong's half-brother or half-sister. I've been lying to you.

SAMANTHA STRONG. It's not possible!

JAKE STRONG. I don't even know what's going on any more!

VALENCIO. Many years ago I employed a frail young girl, a spy, if you will, to infiltrate Jake Strong's home and bring me the one thing that he loved more than anything else.

JAKE STRONG. My teddy bear.

VALENCIO. Even more. The girl's name I employed…Sequoiya. And she succeeded, and brought me…a little baby girl.

(*He strokes* SAMANTHA's *cheek.*)

SAMANTHA STRONG. That means…

VALENCIO. Your real name is neither Sebastian or Samantha. Your real name, my dear, is Jessica Strong. You are Jake's long-lost daughter!

JAKE STRONG. Noooooooooo!

KAITLIN. CUT!

(Lights change.)

That's a wrap everyone.

KERI. Yay! Meet here tomorrow!

JOHN. All right.

TYLER. You know, after today, I'm excited about coming to work.

AMY. Me too.

KERI. Good, because as producer, there are going to be a lot of changes around here...

MORRIS. Starting with no more murders?

KERI. *(Laughing:)* Well...it is going to raise ratings. Good Night everyone!

(Everyone leaves, leaving KERI alone on stage, smiling.)

All right, you can get up now.

(MILES comes back in.)

MILES. Thanks. I can't believe everyone bought that slow knife thing.

KERI. I know. They're pretty stupid.

MILES. Pretty stupid.

KERI. Well—

MILES. I guess I'll lay low for a while—go to Mexico—get some facial reconstruction, perhaps go into a career even more evil...like movie producing.

KERI. Yes.

MILES. You'll do a great job producing the show— But this is the last time I cover up a quadruple murder for you, honey.

KERI. Thanks! You're the best Dad ever.

(They hug.)

Happy ending.

(Lights down.)

End of play

Also available at Playscripts, Inc.

Is He Dead?
by Mark Twain
adapted by David Ives

Comedy
105–120 minutes
4 females, 7 males (11–16 actors possible: 4–6 females, 7–12 males)

Jean-François Millet, a young painter of genius, is in love with Marie Leroux but in debt to a villainous picture-dealer, Bastien André. André forecloses on Millet, threatening debtor's prison unless Marie marries him. Millet realizes that the only way he can pay his debts and keep Marie from marrying André is to die, as it is only dead painters who achieve fame and fortune. Millet fakes his death and prospers, all while passing himself off as his own sister, the Widow Tillou. Now a rich "widow," he must find a way to get out of a dress, return to life, and marry Marie.

Every Christmas Story Ever Told (And Then Some!)
by Michael Carleton, James FitzGerald, and John K. Alvarez
music by Will Knapp

Comedy
80–95 minutes
3 actors (gender flexible)

Instead of performing Charles Dickens' beloved holiday classic for the umpteenth time, three actors decide to perform every Christmas story ever told—plus Christmas traditions from around the world, seasonal icons from ancient times to topical pop-culture, and every carol ever sung. A madcap romp through the holiday season!

Order online at: **www.playscripts.com**

> Also available at Playscripts, Inc.

Miss Nelson is Missing!
adapted by Jeffrey Hatcher

Comedy
60–75 minutes
4 females, 6 males

Miss Nelson can't control her crazy classroom because she's just too nice. But when she disappears, her replacement is the hard-as-nails, detention-loving, recess-canceling, homework-overloading substitute teacher Viola Swamp! With the Big Test approaching, the kids suddenly realize how much they miss Miss Nelson and they'll do anything—including hiring a private eye—to solve the mystery of her disappearance and bring her back.

The Shakespeare Stealer
adapted by Gary L. Blackwood

Historical Drama for young audiences
90–110 minutes
3 females, 12 males, 3 either
(9-18 actors possible: 2-6 females, 7-15 males)

In 1601, a Yorkshire orphan skilled in shorthand (and in lying) is hired by a mysterious stranger to steal the script of *Hamlet*. But when he inadvertently becomes part of Shakespeare's acting troupe, he begins to reconsider his assignment… (A one-act version of this play is also available.)

Order online at: **www.playscripts.com**